OWN YOUR DESTINY

Own Your Destiny

EBENEZER AGBOOLA

The Agboola Ministries

Contents

Dedication   vii
Introduction   ix

1	Destiny	1
2	Find Yourself	51
3	Stay in Your Lane	81
4	The Strategy of the Devil	105
5	Conclusion	150

New Believer's Prayer   155
Contact the Author   157
About the Book   159
Other Books By the Author   161
About The Author   162

Own Your Destiny
Copyright © 2022 by Ebenezer Agboola

All rights reserved. No part of this book may be reproduced in any manner whatsoever without written permission except in the case of brief quotations embodied in critical articles and reviews.

All scripture quotes are taken from the New King James Version (NKJV), Copyright © 1982 Thomas Nelson. All rights reserved.

Scripture quotes marked (KJV) are taken from the King James Version of the Bible.

Scripture quotations are taken from the Holy Bible, New Living Translation, copyright ©1996, 2004, 2007, 2013, 2015 by Tyndale House Foundation. Used by permission of Tyndale House Publishers, Inc., Carol Stream, Illinois 60188. All rights reserved.

ISBN: 978-1-7775-0298-0 (sc)
ISBN: 978-1-7775-0299-7 (e)

Cover Design by Shimoma Kizito.

All rights reserved. No part of this book may be reproduced in any manner whatsoever without written permission except in the case of brief quotations embodied in critical articles and reviews.

First Printing, 2022

Dedication

To the triune God. The Father of my Lord, thank you for creating me with a purpose. My Lord and Savior, Jesus Christ, your death on the cross made destiny easily achievable. I am eternally grateful for your sacrifice. My ever-present help, the Holy Spirit. Your instructions and directions are why destiny is found and achieved. Thank you.

To my spiritual father, Pastor Emmanuel Adewusi. Thank you for being a vessel of honor. The core of this book was born from many of your teachings. The doors you opened have been a trough of many revelations. May the almighty God continue to water you in Jesus' name. Amen.

To my wife, Tumininu Agboola, you are indeed a God-ordained helpmate. Your continuous support means so much to me. I am grateful to God for such a blessing that you are. I love you.

Thank you so much to every individual used by God to bring this vision to life. May the hand of God continue to increase upon your life.

To every individual aiming to please God by walking in their destiny, may the Lord enlighten you as you read on in Jesus' name. Amen.

Introduction

Everyone that God made, He created with a purpose, and no one sets out to not fulfill this purpose. But history has shown us many great examples of people who do precisely that. The Bible made us understand, in Matthew 24:13, that he who endures to the end will be saved. So, starting well is never the issue but standing till the end is where the challenges are. From biblical accounts to today, the examples of those that failed are numerous. Ecclesiastes 1:9 declares that there is nothing new under the sun. Based on this scripture, the devil does not have any new trick rolled up in his sleeve. If we allow God to open our eyes, we will see a pattern in all the devil's attacks. However, we must not forget that the devil has had lots of practice and years to perfect his crafts. Therefore, by studying history and with the help of the Holy Spirit, we can learn from those ahead. As we will see from our studies, there is a common theme among those who fail: distractions. From Judas (John 12:6) to Gehazi (2 Kings 5:20-24) and Demas (2 Timothy 4:10), the common denominator was distractions. Thus, we must avoid this killer to make it and fulfill God's purpose for our life.

This devil's device becomes especially critical and effective in this current age because of the rise of social media, entertainment, fashion, technology, and subtle demonic patronage (palm reading, new age, ungodly meditations, et al.). The avenue for distractions is endless. We may assume that, as Christians, we are good, but we must understand that we are the devil's target. He doesn't waste time on those he already has, the unbelievers. From 2 Corinthians 11:14, we know that the devil always seeks ways to disguise lies as the truth. Since many will not jump in bed with the devil if they know who he is. With this many options, the possibility for distraction is endless, and with this, even Christians may fall (1 Corinthians 10:12). Hence the criticality of our studies here.

As we journey through our studies, we will see that some things are not sin per se. However, doing what we are not supposed to do means not doing what we ought to do. As such, we are distracted, and our destiny—calling will lag for at least the duration spent on the distraction.

I have termed this device a killer because of the pattern and the targets it seeks—to sever a person from their maker, God's plan. And as per Mark 9:40, if you are not for God, you're against Him. Leaving God's plan for anything else is not on God's side. David fell out of God's plan in 2 Samuel 11 and paid dearly for that distraction. By leaving God's plan for even a second, a person can be cut off from the source of life, dead to God in the spirit, and a slave to the devil. As per John 10:10, we know that the devil is the killer; distractions are of the devil. Though sometimes they might seem like "a good cause," we will see in our studies that these are surgically created and designed with precision to destroy a specific person's destiny.

Therefore, this book is valuable as it uncovers another deceptive trick of the devil to steal, kill, and destroy. Yes, these killers might be different for each of us, but they all have their source in the devil with the same goal—to steal, kill and destroy. Thus, wisdom is needed to win this fight like every devil's attack. And since wisdom is defined as the correct application of knowledge, we must have the proper knowledge. To achieve this aim, we must first understand what destinies are. Such will help us to understand why it must be guarded and protected. Secondly, we must know what distraction means and how to avoid it. It's a necessity for our lives and our walk with God.

Before we continue this journey, please say this prayer: Father, open the eyes of my understanding and give me even more profound revelations as it pertains to me in Jesus' name. Amen.

Chapter 1

Destiny

If we are going to uncover the actual effect of distractions, we must understand what it aims to kill. It is especially true because some believe what will be will be no matter what. They live in this state of delusion, where king Solomon found himself towards the end of his life. Such is not just dangerous, but living by this logic is a gross misinterpretation of life, and going through life with this mindset opens the door for the demonic derailment of a person's life.

God, as the creator, has a purpose for all He created. However, He has distinguished humans by giving each of us free will. He did because God created males and females in His image (Genesis 1:26). This implies that each gets to chart their course. Therefore, person A wants red and person B wants green. For example, though essential and critical for eternal life with God, it is still required that a person willingly make their own choice to be saved by God through Jesus (Romans 10:9-10).

God has set a very achievable goal, a target, for each one of us based on what He knows He's placed in you and me. He did not stop here but also recommended a path to achieve it. However, we still have to decide how to go about it. Let us affirm this logic from the creation of man.

Then God said, "Let Us make man in Our image, according to Our likeness; let them have dominion over the fish of the sea, over the birds of the air, and over the cattle, over all the earth and over every creeping thing that creeps on the earth." Genesis 1:26.

From the scripture above, God voiced out His purpose for creating man. "To have dominion over all that was created." The plural form of the statement "let them" shows that this was the goal for the first man—Adam and all that will come from him. We will discuss this thoroughly soon.

Then the Lord God took the man and put him in the garden of Eden to tend and keep it. And the Lord God commanded the man, saying, "Of every tree of the garden you may freely eat; but of the tree of the knowledge of good and evil you shall not eat, for in the day that you eat of it you shall surely die." Genesis 2:15-17.

Next, God put Adam in the garden and on a path to achieving that goal. The path was to tend, keep the garden and avoid the tree of knowledge and evil. If this is followed, Adam is guaranteed to achieve the goal set before him.

So, when the woman saw that the tree was good for food, that it was pleasant to the eyes, and a tree desirable to make one wise, she took of its fruit and ate. She also gave it to her husband, and he ate. Genesis 3:6.

Here we saw that the man under the woman's influence exercised his free will and made a choice contrary to God's recommendations. To put this in a relatable way, a teacher will show the students the expectation(s) for an exam. However, it is still up to each student to follow that recommendation during the exam. For those that followed, success is inevitable; for others, success is not guaranteed.

Since God is both the creator (Isaiah 45:18) and the judge (Isaiah 33:22) of all, thus the teacher in our analogy, it is wise to inquire of Him to decipher this goal. Though there are other ways to figure this out, this is the most logical and the best way to generate the correct result. We have the confidence for the right information through this route. It will help us avoid assumptions and disappointments. It is also the only way to get our purpose's totality and the proper reward afterwards.

God does not cause accidents. Like Adam, placing us here on earth, in particular families and situations, has something, if not everything, to do with our destinies. We must know the purpose God has set for us to achieve and the pathway we must follow. These questions and many more are what we will examine next.

What is Destiny?

Destiny is God's ordained purpose for one to fulfill and achieve while here on earth. It is the purpose or intent set by God for a person. As seen in our previous discussion, God spoke about us and put us here on earth to fulfill what He has said about us. Therefore, there is a goal and a recommended path for everyone.

Many assume that since destiny is something God has ordained, it must come to pass. They say it must happen regardless of what we do or don't do. This mentality is not just wrong but doesn't consider the existence of our free will. The Bible made us understand that God knocks on the door of our hearts to gain access to transform our life

(Revelation 3:20). There are no circumstances under heaven where we will see God force Himself on anyone. The individual or their authority must allow it. Some still do not believe in God because it is their choice. It is the devil and his cohort that force their will on another. God wants us to choose Him willingly.

Another important fact here is this: since humans exist within time, there is, therefore, a time factor for all we do during our physical lifetime (Ecclesiastes 3). So, we can deduce that our purpose will also exist within the function of time. As such, we will be required to do certain things at a particular time to achieve God's ordained goals. However, if we have messed things up or missed some time factors, the good news is that God doesn't exist within time and, as such, He can restore (Joel 2:25). It is never too late to align with the concepts of this book.

Like Adam, the instructions given to an individual by God are the best pathway to fulfilling the individual destiny set by God.

From Deuteronomy 10:13, we can deduce that we are to keep the command of God for our good. Using this scripture, we can say that fulfilling destiny as ordained and prescribed by God will carry its reward. Also, we know that the devil would not seek to destroy something that isn't crucial, beneficial, and critical to our walk with God.

We are placed on earth to fulfill destiny; there are rewards while here and after living for a job well done. From Matthew 25:14-30, we can infer that fulfilling destiny as ordained by God will increase trust both from God to us and from us to God. As per Hebrews 9:27, judgment is next once our time on earth is over. I believe from the scriptures that there are two stages of evaluation that we will go through afterlife—Salvation and Destiny. Salvation from the sense of accepting God's redemptive work through Jesus (Romans 10:9-10) and destiny (the reason for our existence)—these are the works referred to in Revelations 20:12. Thus, we will all be judged as per our faith in God through Jesus and our works, that is, fulfilling destiny. From John 3:16, we see that salvation gives us access to eternal life in heaven. And from Matthew 6:20, we can deduce that fulfilling destiny adds treasure to this eternal life. It makes it possible to store up treasures in heaven. Salvation gives us a pleasant home with God after life. But fulfilling destiny as prescribed by God helps us to furnish this home.

In summary, destiny is simply the plan of God for an individual. It is why we were created and placed here on earth. Fulfilling defines an individual as a success or a failure from God's point of view. Genesis 3 and Genesis 6:6 (*And the Lord was sorry that He had made man on the earth, and He was grieved in His heart*) give us an insight into God's heart when we fail to fulfil destiny in His way. We grieve our creator by simply not fulfilling destiny.

INDIVIDUAL DESTINIES

In Jeremiah 1:5, God spelled out Jeremiah's destiny. *"Before I formed you in the womb, I knew you; Before you were born, I sanctified you; I ordained you a prophet to the nations."* This purpose was set for him by God and hence Jeremiah's destiny. In the same way, God has an ordained goal for me and you. From 1 Corinthians 14:33, we know God does not do accidents but instead brings about very well-thought-out orchestrated incidents. Therefore, *all things work together for good to those who love God, to those who are called according to His purpose* (Romans

8:28). Before Adam was created, God spoke and thought about him (Genesis 1:26).

Similarly, God followed the same pattern before Eve was created (Genesis 2:18). Based on this fact, I can assure you that you are not an accident; God thought and spoke about you before you were formed in your mother's womb. He knows you by the name He called you. The dire circumstances that may surround your birth have nothing to do with God's plan for your life (Jeremiah 29:11). You were conceived and born when God ordained it. To put this in perspective, if Bill Gates weren't born when he was born, our world would have been affected in a way we cannot even imagine. Only God, who knows the future, can perfectly plan the right time for people to be born. Bill Gates was conceived, born, and he grew to different stages at just the right time to make a lasting impact in the world. God is a strategic God. Your birth was strategic to your impact and destiny. God knitted you together in the womb (Psalm 139:13) at the right time with a purpose in mind. You are not on the earth because your parents made a mistake but because God placed you here for a goal only you can achieve.

Furthermore, your fingerprint is one of a kind. There is no other person on the earth with your fingerprint. Such is a testament to the fact that you were created specially by God for a specific purpose (Psalm 139:14). You are different, unique, and needed; without you in the world right now, the world as we know it will not be the same. But, unfortunately, these are facts that the devil doesn't want us to know.

From the analysis above, we can tell that knowing our purpose is necessary. Low self-esteem, pride, fear, and many of life's identity issues can be traced to an unknown purpose. It makes so much sense because we are here for a purpose. We cannot enjoy life or make any lasting impact until we align with that purpose. Are you frustrated with life? Are you feeling useless? Are you thinking of killing yourself? Are you not making progress in life? Are you not enjoying life? Are you anxious, fearful, and scared always? These phenomena and many more can indicate that such individuals are not in their purpose. But as we will see in our studies, there is still time. God can still align and restore us on track.

God likes diversity, and as such, He has wired us differently to fulfil a different purposes. However, life will be frustrating and only fulfilling once we fall in place, that is, in our allocated space in the puzzle.

Since we are alive, the devil failed in his quest to kill us in the womb. Therefore, his following action prevents us from discovering our God-ordained purpose in life. The late Dr. Myles Monroe said that if one's purpose is unknown, abuse is inevitable. The abuse of anything or anyone indicates a lack of purpose. Many abuses themselves and others because of a lack of purpose. For example, many abuse their body with food, drugs, and substances because they do not know or fully grasp their purpose. Such is an avenue for satanic bondages, such as harmful addictions, bad cravings, et al., and hence fulfilling its mission—to kill, steal, and destroy. If we figure out our purpose, the devil doesn't just stop pursuing us; he instead sends distractions which we will discuss in this book. But first, let's drill deeper into destinies and discover God's ordination for each of us.

In the beginning

In Genesis 1:1, the Bible says, "*in the beginning, God created the heavens and the earth.*" Isaiah 44:24 says, "*Thus, the LORD, your Redeemer, And He who formed you from the womb: "I am the LORD, who makes all things, who stretches out the heavens all alone, Who spreads abroad the earth by Myself.*" The statements of these scriptures made it abundantly clear that God is the creator of all things. Yes, God made many things that we do not understand their necessity or function. For example, the human appendix is still a piece of the puzzle we are yet to piece together. But here is one sure thing: from 1 Corinthians 14:33, we know that God is not the author of confusion. Ecclesiastes 3:1 established that there is a season for everything. And Romans 8:28 affirms that all things work together for good. These scriptures and many others testify that there is no accident with God. Using this logic, we can deduce that God made all things for a purpose, as established earlier. Therefore, it only makes sense that if we are to understand the reason behind all that God has made, we will have to ask Him. This purpose and many more will help us utilize what God has made for its intentions.

Since God is love and due to His merciful nature, He has put some things in us that, if we observe, we can deduce portions of our destiny without being in God or consulting Him. For example, though God is the ultimate healer, He has made an avenue for those with little faith and especially unbelievers, to still get healing via medical science without actively consulting Him. However, this does not negate Him. Just as medical science still does not know it all or has cures for all ailments, it is impossible to deduce the entirety of our destiny without God. Earlier, we established that God is the Maker of all, and He predestined us. In this way, we see that humans cannot know the totality of destiny, and success is unachievable without God. This means that whatever we know or achieve without God, though it might seem reasonable, fulfilling and right, will still be deemed a failure (Mark 8:36). Even if we get to know some of our destiny outside of God, we must fulfill it based on God's ordained path to achieve success and ensure nothing is left behind. The totality of our destiny is reserved to be known and attained in God.

Earlier, we vaguely alluded to the time factor of our destiny. It is because God doesn't tell us or show us the entirety of our destiny at once. The enormity of God's plan for us and our maturity, often based on time, makes this impossible to grasp. But instead, one step at a time (Isaiah 28:10).

To truly understand our purpose in life, we must go back to the beginning of all life. From the beginning, we saw in Genesis 1:26 that we are all created in the image of God to have dominion on earth. As such, we are gods on earth (Psalm 82:6); this implies that there is a lot in us. God decorated us all with fantastic potential. We are containers of unfathomable possibilities. It is our destiny.

To explain this further, let us look at a weird incident in Matthew 15:26-27. *But He (Jesus) answered and said, "It is not good to take the children's bread and throw it to the little dogs." And she said, "Yes, Lord, yet even the little dogs eat the crumbs which fall from their masters' table."* The woman in this story wanted a miracle, but Jesus stating the fact made it quite clear that His hands were tied because what she was asking was reserved for those in God. However, the woman clapped back with a fascinating response. Her response has been a source of strength for me since I discovered it. She challenged Jesus by saying *"that what she wanted is crumb compared to what God has for His own."* So, we can conclude from this biblical account that whatever we see an unbeliever achieve are simply crumbs compared to what God set on the table before those in Him (Psalm 23:5). In this way, we see that what a person discovers as their destiny outside of God cannot be the entirety of it. It is nothing compared to what God made them to achieve. However, the totality of this enormous destiny can only be seen, discovered, and attained only in God. Therefore, what an unbeliever gains or has does not affect me because I know what I have access to is way more than that. It is because the *eye has not seen, heard, nor entered the heart of man the things God has prepared for those who love Him* (1 Corinthians 2:9).

Due to this enormous nature of our destiny, God will show us our purpose, *precept upon precept, Line upon Line, Line upon Line, here a little, there a little."* (Isaiah 28:10). He does this based on time and seasons (Ecclesiastes 3:1), which often contribute to our maturity. Thus, we see that whatever we discover outside of God is only a tip of an enormous iceberg compared to what God has put in us.

At the end of our life, we will be judged based on God's passing grade for us individually, not anything else or our assumptions. We see an insight into this in Matthew 25:14-30. Therefore, coming to God through Jesus is crucial; otherwise, everything we achieve here on earth is a waste. There is no way to accomplish all God destined for us without God. If you would like to make that decision –

connecting with God, stop reading now and say the new believer's prayer at the end of the book.

Mini-Destinies

Since destiny is a big goal that will ideally span throughout our life, we imagine that there will be a lot of small goals on the path to achieving the primary goal. These small goals are what I have termed mini destinies. These are the leading goals to the main destiny. These are what many can deduce outside of God. With patterns, observation, and passions, we can deduce mini destinies without God.

Fulfilling the mini destinies does not connote success. It simply shows that we are on the right path to fulfilling the goal. And unless we come to God, we will never fulfil the primary purpose.

Due to the nature of humans, we exist within time. Therefore, we will be allowed to see a destination to achieve within that time frame at a different time. It becomes our primary focus; passion, love, and energy cling to that destination, but it is never the overall goal. It is simply a pitstop on our way to the destination. Therefore, Apostle Paul functioned as an evangelist at one point, a teacher at another and so on. It doesn't mean that God was confused but instead walking Paul's steps towards fulfilling His overall destiny. From Acts 9:15 (*But the Lord said to him, "Go, for he is a chosen vessel of Mine to bear My name before Gentiles, kings, and the children of Israel*), it is pretty clear that Paul's main destiny was to challenge the status quo and make Jesus known in a unique way to all. All he did through many mini destinies that led him to fulfil this (2

Timothy 4:7). He was focusing on this goal all through his days (Philippians 3:14). Until this was fulfilled, there was no release to die (Philippians 1:23-24). In straightforward terms, for as long as we are alive here on earth, we are on the way to fulfilling our ultimate destiny. Ideally, the day God allowed us to die and all things being equal, that is the day we may have fulfilled our primary purpose here.

Unfortunately, these mini destinies are what many people know and pursue. The danger here is that once the time allocated lapses, such people become useless and unfulfilled. All the feelings of lack of purpose will return. They will lose their drive and hence lose their purpose for life. The mini destinies must not be confused with distractions—which we will examine in detail in the subsequent sections.

A classic example was King Solomon. From 1 Chronicles 28:6, we see that God destined King Solomon to be a builder for Him. As such, He started passionately and built the temple of God for seven years (1 Kings 6:37-38). Once the time for this mini destiny lapsed, the force of his main destiny— to build kept on pushing instead of asking God what to build next. The devil hijacked it, and he focused on his palace (selfishness) and built it for 13 years (1 Kings 7:1). He continued that path and built at least 700 shrines for his foreign women (1 Kings 11:8-9). We see that King Solomon lost interest in life, and his writings in Ecclesiastes show his frame of mind towards the end. His primary purpose was to establish (build) the kingdom of God on earth. Such is a lifetime job; instead, he engaged in one mini destiny and stopped there. As we saw, he continued building (establishing), that is, engaging in mini destinies, but he was unfulfilled, as seen in his writings. Therefore, whatever you are involved in that brings you the feeling of unfulfillment is a red flag that you have engaged in something that doesn't align with your main destiny. The point here is that mini-destinies are not the main destiny. The main destiny will always push us like it did King Solomon, and the minis should always align and accumulate to fulfil the main destiny.

We must never assume to know the main because of the patterns shown by the minis. As we have established, only God can unequivocally affirm the main destiny. So, a God factor in every destiny (main and mini) must be located; otherwise, the devil can hijack it.

In summary, since God predestined us, He is the only one who knows and decides our main destiny. Until God tells us we are done here on earth, we must never assume to know or understand the main destiny. For as long as we are alive on earth, we must treat any goal set before us by God as a mini destiny. We must run passionately to achieve it and always return to God once it is done or the time-lapse (i.e., the feeling of unfulfillment returns, among many other things). It is the only way we can keep running toward God for the rest of our days and avoid distractions.

THE NEW TESTAMENT MINI-DESTINIES

From the account of the Bible in Genesis 1, man was the last creation of God before He rested. From the statement that precedes the creation of man, it was pretty clear that God made the earth for man. So, it makes sense that God gave man dominion over the earth (Genesis 1:26). Dominion is, therefore, every man's (male and female) individual destiny. These destinies were expressed in many different diversities. But due to carelessness, the first man lost this destiny to the devil (Genesis 3 & Luke 4:6). Therefore, instead of man, the devil became the god of this world (2 Corinthians 4:4). However, God in His infinite mercies and love has sent Jesus to reclaim this dominion and refine our destinies (John 3:16 & John 10:10). This Jesus did when He died for our sin and took back what the devil stole from us (Matthew 28:18).

*But to each one of us, grace was given according to the measure of Christ's gift. Therefore, He says: "When He ascended on high, He led captivity captive, and **gave gifts to men.**" (Now this, "He ascended"—what does it mean but that **He also first descended into the lower parts of the earth? He who descended is also the One who ascended far above all the heavens, that He might fill all things.) And He Himself gave some to be apostles, some prophets, some evangelists, and some pastors and teachers,** for the equipping of the saints for the work of ministry, for the edifying of the body of Christ, till we all come to the unity of the faith and of the knowledge of the Son of God, to a perfect man, to the measure of the stature of the fullness of Christ; that we should no longer be children, tossed to and fro and carried about with every wind of doctrine, by the trickery of men, in the cunning craftiness of deceitful plotting, but, speaking the truth in love, may grow up in all things into Him who is the head—Christ—from whom the whole body, joined and knit together by what every joint supplies, according to the effective working by which every part does its share, causes growth of the body for the edifying of itself in love.* (Ephesians 4:7-16)

The scriptures above gave us an insight into what God did through the work of Jesus. The first thing we will discuss from this scripture verse is that *when Jesus ascended high, He led captivity captive and gave gifts to men (male and female).* Naturally, it is assumed that Christians (the ones that come to God through Jesus) are the ones that will have access to such gifts. But the nature of the statement here connotes something different. Something I learnt from my spiritual father. Men mean all men. Not just Christians or churchgoers but all men. But why would Jesus give gifts to everyone, including unbelievers? The answer to this question can be found in Romans 5:8 (*but God demonstrates His own love toward us, in that while we were still sinners, Christ died for us*) and John 3:16 (*For God so loved the world that He gave His only begotten Son, that whoever believes in Him should not perish but have everlasting life*). These scriptures show that the restorative gifts from Jesus' redemptive work on the cross came to all men before any man became born again. God did this out of love, for God is love (1 John 4:8).

By the work of Jesus on the cross, descending into the lower parts of the earth and ascending in victory, He restored men to their original state. We were reinstated to the way God envisioned us in Eden's garden, in the beginning, that is, to have dominion on earth (See Revelations 5:10). You might argue that only those saved should have access to the redemptive gifts listed in Ephesians 4. But God made Adam have dominion before he could even choose God. In the same way, God sent Jesus to restore sovereignty to humanity before we can accept Jesus. So, the gift of Jesus to men has nothing to do with whether a man is born again or not. Even salvation is made available to all because of Jesus' work. Today, every man has a variant of these redemptive gifts of Jesus in them. Glory to God!

Since these gifts originated from Jesus in the New Testament, it is only reasonable to say that the full potential and success of these gifts are obtainable only through Jesus. Adam had the destiny of dominion but went about it in his way and failed (Genesis 3). In the same way, the gift of Jesus will only produce the best when we follow the path of Jesus, that is, to come to Jesus through salvation. To accept Jesus as our personal Lord and savior. If you'd like to receive Jesus, say the prayer of salvation at the end of the book now.

The Options

The next thing we will explore from Ephesians 4 is that *He (Jesus) Himself gave some to be apostles, some prophets, some evangelists, and some pastors and teachers.* Within these five giftings is where everybody's variant of giftings can be found. The Christians called these the fivefold ministry or the five offices. It is described as such because, in any assembly of God, you will find these five distinct offices on display.

As noted by Jesus in Matthew 25:14-30, some individuals might be in one office while others may be in multiple offices. Such is solely dependent on the giver of the gifts, our assignments and how He has created and wired us. We will explore these more when we discuss the offices. But since these giftings are for all men, we must understand that wherever men gather, we'll find these offices and their variants on display.

There is a concept that we must discuss before we proceed to explore each gift. We have established that Jesus gave gifts to all. Implies that we will find some of these gifts in and outside the church. The unbelievers will most certainly utilize their gifts outside the church, but are believers restricted to the church? The answer to this question depends on the situation.

Let's explore this even further. From Revelations 1:6 (and *has made us kings and priests to His God and Father, to Him be glory and dominion forever and ever. Amen.)* and Revelations 5:10 (*And have made us kings and priests to our God; And we shall reign on the earth.)*, we see that Jesus did restore us to the primary goal of our creation in the beginning—to reign over the earth and have dominion (Genesis 1:26). This affirmed what we'd discussed earlier. But from the scripture, we noticed that the path to this restored dominion is through Kingship and Priesthood. You will find the five offices in each of these dominion streams. There is every gift (the five offices) of Jesus in the kingship and priesthood streams. As believers, we follow the path of Jesus and have subscribed to His works, so we have both natures (kings and priests) in us as per the scriptures. What this truly means, we will explore in the similarity section. But for now, we can say that any of the gifts of Jesus in a believer can be used in any dominion stream as deemed fit by God. Unlike unbelievers, we're genuinely not restricted to one stream. But we have our primary stream.

We will be discussing the kings and priests even further, but for right now, let us consider this simple fact. If you are reading this, it means you are alive. What this implies is that you are alive in the world. If you are a believer, you also belong to the body of Christ (1 Corinthians 12:27). In simple terms, God expects you to be a king in the world and, at the very least, a priest to the world as a child of God (2 Corinthians 5:20). Glory to God! Therefore, Apostle Peter called a child of God a royal (king) priesthood (1 Peter 2:9). Otherwise, we'll be restricted to just one stream—either a king or a priest. Such is the state of an unbeliever. In that, if an unbeliever works hard and hustles hard, they may attain kingship, that is, reach the height of their career (dominion), be a subject matter expert and a force to reckon with in that field (though that is only possible due to the work of Jesus). However, such individuals can never attain priesthood by work. Priests are vessels chosen and separated by God through salvation. Works can propel to kingship, but the priesthood is sacred and exclusive. God has separated the priests to be soigné for His purposes. With all that in mind, let us dig deeper into these two streams of dominion.

The King

A king, as per Google, is *the ruler of an independent state, especially one who inherits the position by right of birth*. From this definition, there are a few things to consider. First, a king rules over a state, which is a domain. Such qualifies the kingship as the first realm of dominion. But we must remember that a king only has rule/dominion over his kingdom. This concept becomes extremely critical in Chapter 3. But for now, all we need to know is that any king's honor and respect in their domain is not guaranteed when such a king crosses to any other domain.

Secondly, the phrase "*especially one who inherits the position by right of birth*" affirms what we had discussed earlier. In our world, most individuals often become royal by no works of their own. But instead by the sacrifices of their ancestors. In the same way, we have all the giftings to attain kingship not because we receive Jesus but because Jesus died for all humans. So, everyone can be royal since Jesus died for all (2 Corinthians 5:15). However, being a royal doesn't make you one. There are paths to be one that must be followed (Proverbs 22:29). Otherwise, a royal can end up a pauper.

The path highlighted here to attain this right of rulership is by birth. From the accounts of the Bible, God owns it all (Psalm 24:1). As per Hebrews 1:1-2 (*God, who at various times and in various ways spoke in time past to the fathers by the prophets, has in these last days spoken to us by His Son, whom He has appointed heir of all things, through whom also He made the worlds*), Jesus has been appointed the heir of all. Since Jesus and God are one (John 10:30), Jesus owns it all. Everything was made through Jesus because He is the word of God personified (John 1:1-3 & Colossian 1:16). And since God spoke creation into existence (Genesis 1:3), all were created through Jesus. Thus, to truly attain the height that God created us for, we must be born into God's family, that is, to belong to the household of God (Ephesians 2:19 & 1 John 5:4).

You may say, but I have seen an unbeliever ruling. How can that be? Such is possible for a few reasons. But I'll only highlight one for the sake of our study. As mentioned earlier, a royal that doesn't know what's theirs and follows the path can end up a pauper. As established, all men are designed to be royalty (Genesis 1:26). But those in Christ are enhanced to be at the very top of the dominion that God envisioned at the beginning. So, they are equipped even to achieve more due to the advantage of the Holy Spirit. As such, believers are senior royals because of the work of Jesus and their subscription to it. This grants access to the Holy Spirit, who will make them senior royals (Acts 2:38).

With the Holy Spirit, we are equipped even more to rule; it is our natural habitat because we are God's priority

(Zachariah 2:8). But if a believer doesn't know this fact, non-royals, that is, unbelievers can rule over them and in their place. For example, we saw in Luke 16:19-31 a seemingly enhanced royal called Lazarus who died a pauper. On the other hand, the rich man was wealthy just by what God gave to all men. He was a non-royal who attained height (royalty) through hard work but ruled over a senior royal called Lazarus. Such is so because *God is not mocked; for whatever a man sows, that he will also reap* (Galatians 6:7). Since nature abhors a vacuum, if believers do not take their place at the top and rule, God may allow an unbeliever to rule. Such is especially dangerous because *when the righteous (senior royals) are in authority, the people rejoice; But when a wicked man rules, the people groan* (Proverbs 29:2, emphasis added). We all benefit the most only when believers assume the top and rule. Therefore, an unbeliever at the top indicates believers' negligence. The moment we become born again, we become co-heir with Jesus (Romans 8:17), we are senior royalties of the earth, and as such, we are to rule. To rule is ours by right of birth (being born again). Thereby restoring Genesis 1:26. Glory to God!

Due to the nature of this royalty—to rule on the earth, those called to rule in this manner often do so outside the church. For example, Joseph ruled over all of Egypt (Genesis 41:37-44). Daniel ruled in Babylon (Daniel 2:48). So, such people are often in positions of power and influence, like CEOs, Entrepreneurs, Government officials etc.

The Priest

Priests are an exclusive group of people. Unlike the kings, the priests, as seen from the beginning in Exodus

28:1 & Deuteronomy 18:5, are chosen by God. They are purified, set apart and must follow specific prescriptions God sets. From the scriptures, we see that these are today's Christians (1 Peter 2:9 & Titus 2:14). Now, as per Hebrews 10:25, if we are of God, though we may be senior royal in the world, we also must belong to the church.

We must understand that though God chose the children of Levi to minister unto Him (Deuteronomy 18:5), only Aaron's lineage was ordained as high priests (Exodus 28:1). From the scriptures, we see that the high priests as ordained by God are the equivalent of kings in this realm. So, there are two options within the Priesthood. The high priests, I will call the senior royals of this domain, while the Priests are the junior royals. Remember, since God chooses both, they are royals. Aaron's lineage is appointed to be at the top by this calling. Therefore, all Christians are priests and, thereby, royals, but within this are some individuals who God calls into ministry—these are the high priests, the senior royals.

The need for a different stream of dominion in the church is because the Church of Christ is a spiritual home. It is an exclusive domain for the chosen ones of God. As such, a different governing system is essential. As the earth is a home for humanity and other species, the church is a home for the children of God. Therefore, God built/created heaven and the earth (Genesis 1:1), and Jesus *built the Church* (Matthew 16:18). Yes, there is a physical building on earth, but the church is a spiritual phenomenon. When building the church of old, God told Moses, "*See to it that you make them according to the pattern which was shown you on the mountain*" Exodus 25:40. From Hebrews 8:5, we see that the church is an expression of the heavenly temple, this even corroborates the point that the church is a domain on its own. As such, those called to rule within the church are the royals of this domain, called Priests. Due to the nature of this domain, there are no non-royals, just the senior and the junior royals.

Merriam-Webster defines a priest as *one authorized to perform a religion's sacred rites, especially as a mediatory agent between humans and God.* From this definition, we will look at a few things. First, a priest must be authorized. From the Old Testament tabernacles, we saw God Himself appoint the priests. In the same way today, Jesus authorized and gifted the priests of today. Jesus is the builder of the church and authorizes the rulers—Priests. Therefore, from Ephesians 4, it was Christ that gave these gifts. From the Old Testament, we know that God instructed Moses to build a tabernacle so He could dwell among them (Exodus 25:8). Solomon later transformed this tabernacle concept into a temple during His days (1 Kings 6). In both cases, God built His dwelling here on earth by deciding who and how to build it.

Secondly, the Priest mediates between God and humans. In this capacity, God expects all priests (Christians) to function in the worldly domain and the high priests to the priests in the church realm.

Since Jesus and God are one (John 10:30), God built the church today (Matthew 16:18). As such, the Church is God's dwelling today. So, it is only reasonable for all of God's children to be found where God dwells. In that case, though Jesus is the authority over the Church (Colossians 1:18), He has given the Priesthood delegated authority to rule within the church domain today. With senior royals at the helm of power and junior royals in supportive roles as ordained.

In Hebrews 13:17, the Bible says, "*obey those who rule over you and be submissive, for they watch out for your souls, as those who must give account. Let them do so with joy and not with grief, for that would be unprofitable for you.*" Since kingship does not look over the souls, it is fair to infer that the Bible referred to the Priesthood. The Amplified Bible gave us a clearer insight, affirming this assertion by saying, "*Obey your [spiritual] leaders and submit to them [recognizing their authority over you].*" As such, the church is the domain where priests rule.

The Similarity of Kings and Priests

The main similarity between these streams of dominion is as follows. The kings are rulers primarily in the worldly domain, while the priests are precisely that, primarily in the church realm (Hebrews 13:17). As Children of God, we are in the world physically but alive in the spirit (Romans 8:10). Therefore, we currently exist in the world and the church (the body of Christ). Jesus died so we could have dominion in both. Like Daniel, he can be considered a junior royal in the worldly domain (Daniel 2:48), serving under a king, but a senior ruler in the spiritual domain (Daniel 5:11). He was at the very top of the spiritualists of his time but was third in command in the worldly kingdom. In this way, we are both kings as well as priests. Since Daniel was a senior royal in the priesthood domain, we can say he was a priest first, then a king. Like Daniel, some might find themselves a senior royal in one stream and a junior in the other. Or like King David, whom I deemed a senior royal in both domains. He ruled over Israel (2 Samuel 5:4) and was also a Prophet (Acts 2:30). What we are not permitted to be as Christians is non-royal or die a junior royal in both domains. There is at least a domain within the two where God has ordained us to be senior royal. Locate where and let God help you to the topmost top. The moment we become born again, we are born to rule no matter what. Glory to God!

In this way, a born-again business tycoon under the authority of a local church may be deemed a junior royal in the priesthood but a senior royal in the business world. As such, they must submit and obey those that rule over them within the body of Christ (the high priests) (Hebrews 13:17). But if a born-again business magnate also happens to be a high priest within the body of Christ, we can deem such an individual as a senior royal in both domains.

These two are needed because the world has kings while the body of Christ has priests. Looking at the Bible, we can see that God had these two in every kingdom He established. For every king, there was a priest(s). Though Moses was a senior royal in both domains, He served as the Israelite "king" and priest at the beginning; God still selected a whole tribe separately to be priests unto Him. So, before God ordained the first king of Israel, He established the priesthood. He was indicating the importance of the priesthood. Therefore, though some of us may be a king in the worldly domain, we are still priests at the very same time. We are God's ambassadors in both domains. We are expected to let people know about our God and mediate between God and the non-royals as needed. Among many other things, it is our priestly responsibility to strive to get as many non-royal into the royalty of God (See Mark 16:15). And if we are high priests, we are already priests and kings at the very same time by ruling over God's people (See Hebrews 13:17) and being God's ambassador.

Therefore, a believer called by God to rule in the worldly domain is a king. They will likely do so outside of the church (ruling above non-royals, principalities, and powers in the worldly domains) while submitting to a high priest within the church. In this way, we see that not everyone is called and chosen by God to function within the church; others are elected to function outside the church as kings and queens. Glory to God!

The Offices

We have established that there are also two streams of dominion (Kings and Priests). And that we have rulership in both domains. Therefore, 2 Peter 1:9 called us a "royal priesthood." Jesus came to restore these two rulerships to us after it was stolen from Adam in the garden (Genesis 3). However, as mentioned earlier, each of these streams of dominion has five arms (offices). So, the Priesthood and Kingship have five offices.

Now let us get acquainted with each office from a general point of view. After which, we will bring it all together for a better understanding of their necessities. Due to the nature of the dominion streams, each office may have different names depending on the stream. But the name presented in the Bible is synonymous with Priesthood. So, for example, a Pastor in the Priesthood may not be referred to as that in the Kingship, while a teacher seems to have the same name across the board. Also, the significance and role of each office may differ between streams; but there is a general cord that binds the two streams together, which we will explore further.

Using the order presented in the Bible, we will analyze these offices as follow: *And He Himself gave some to be apostles, some prophets, some evangelists, and some pastors and teachers* (Ephesians 4:11).

The Apostles

A simple search of the word apostle will first and mainly produce a result synonymous with the Priesthood. However, the deeper we go into the research of this word, we will see that it is not just for that. For example, one of the later definitions from Google defines an apostle as *a vigorous and pioneering advocate or supporter of a particular policy, idea, or cause.* Similarly, Merriam-Webster later defines it as *a person who initiates a great moral reform or who first advocates an important belief or system.*

From these two definitions, an apostle is, therefore, a pioneer, the first to catch an idea. By this grace on them, they can lead and occupy leadership positions. They can also manifest their gifting in entrepreneurship, bringing about a new idea.

There was an incident in Acts 6 that we can analyze to understand the Apostle better. Yes, this is from the Priesthood, but as we will see, this is applicable in both dominion streams.

Now in those days, when the number of the disciples was multiplying, there arose a complaint against the Hebrews by the Hellenists, because their widows were neglected in the daily distribution. Then the twelve (apostles) summoned the multitude of the disciples and said, "It is not desirable that we should leave the word of God and serve tables. Therefore, brethren, seek out from among you seven men of good reputation, full of the Holy Spirit and wisdom, whom we may appoint over this business; but we will give ourselves continually to prayer and to the ministry of the word." And the saying pleased the whole multitude. And they chose Stephen, a man full of faith and the Holy Spirit, and Philip, Prochorus, Nicanor, Timon, Parmenas, and Nicolas, a proselyte from Antioch, whom they set before the apostles; and when they had prayed, they laid hands on them. Then the word of God spread, and the number of the disciples multiplied greatly in Jerusalem, and a great many of the priests were obedient to the faith. (Acts 6:1-7, emphasis added).

Looking at the scripture above, we saw two things worth analyzing.

First, though the Apostles were the first to catch the vision to start a thing, they have their limit(s). This office only produces results when they stick to certain things in their domain. As pioneers, the apostles can function in all the offices as needed at the inception of the vision. In the same way, a parent is equipped to serve as everything a child needs at the beginning. However, as the vision grows and expands, the apostolic offices become more and more of a general overseer, chairman or even a Head of state. That is, a person who has the final say determines the route of an organization, country etc. To relate it to our analogy, a child becomes more and more independent of the parent as they grow.

In the same way, the vision becomes more and more independent of the pioneer as it grows. Such is one of the ways that the success of an apostle is measured. In this way, we see many ideas running independently without the pioneer. But just like all things being equal, there is always room for the parent in a child's life, so there is and always will be room for the apostle in the vision's life.

Secondly, after Jesus had left the earth, He left the survival of His established works in the hand of the Apostles. As we can see, after a while, a problem arose. This issue indicated that the apostolic office has now lapsed due to growth. It means that the apostles could do it all before then, as we've explored above. However, once this issue arose, the apostles clarified their core responsibilities. As such, a need for new office gifting arose. Therefore, apostles must understand that everything else they do for the vision is secondary. Just as a parent is not expected to feed a child forever, a time must come when they can feed themselves. Since the apostles are pioneers, the custodian of the vision, keeping the vision alive and ensuring that the vision and mission are or will be achieved is their primary. Therefore, like any good parent, they make suggestions, provide guidance, and make final decisions when needed. This gifting is meant to be the absolute solution provider when all lower tiers of leadership fail. Thus, children are advised to escalate to their parents when they have reached their end in all matters, especially in life and family.

So, an apostle is the parent of a vision. The failure or success of the vision rests on their ability to put the right structures and systems in place and their leadership skills. These are the "natural leaders." Others can learn to enhance their leadership abilities, but these are equipped to lead a vision and bring it to fruition.

Weakness

Many things can constitute weaknesses for an apostle. However, there are two lethal things that we will discuss here. These are pride and offence.

Pride

As incredible as this gift is, we can see that an apostle must watch out for pride. Since it seems as though they are above all and, in some cases, know it all, it can be a slippery slope if the proper measure is not in place because *God resists the proud but gives grace to the humble.* (James 4:6). Therefore, it is not some advice for an apostle to watch out for this killer but rather an absolute necessity. An apostle must remember that they are the only ones that know the vision front and back. Every other person is simply playing catch-up. So, they must resist the temptation of looking down on others simply because they haven't caught the vision.

Offence

Another fatal weakness of this office is offence. The apostles must understand that people enter things for selfish reasons, so some may never catch the vision if their selfish ambition is satisfied. For example, the visionary, the Apostle of the vision, may not necessarily be there to make money but to help humanity. Yes, money will come from their rulership, but that wasn't the primary intent. However, not everyone employed by the company will have the same vision and zeal as the visionary. Some are simply there for their paychecks. If this is being satisfied, they may never desire to catch up to the vision. So, an apostle must make peace with this and not get offended (Luke 17:1). To help us understand further when Jesus was on earth, He was the master apostle, He came for the sake of humanity, but Judas was clearly in it for the wrong reasons (John 12:6).

Judas never catches up to the vision, and this destroys him (Matthew 27:1-5). Moses was a master apostle as well; he was in it to rescue Israel from bondage. But the mixed multitude of Israel was clearly in it for the wrong reasons (Numbers 11:4). In both cases, this was a betrayer, and both Jesus and Moses were able to manage it. Yes, we can train lower-tier leaders to get the right people, but often things like this happen, hence the need for another office. An apostle must be at peace with this fact and avoid offence. To learn more about offence and why you must run from it, please read "The Bait of Satan" by John Bevere.

The Prophets

The importance and significance of this office can be seen and deduced in the fact that every religion has the office of prophets. But as we have explained, this office is not restricted to the religious sphere; it transcends into the kingship realm. Though the name prophet is synonymous with spirituality, we will uncover here that this office has its place in our secular world today. We will see that its importance is the same across the board.

But first, who is a prophet? Let's zoom in on Google's two interesting definitions. First, *a person who advocates or speaks in a visionary way about a new belief, cause, or theory*. Secondly, *a person who makes or claims to be able to make predictions*. From these definitions, we can see why we need a prophet in every sphere of life. We mentioned earlier that an Apostle is a pioneer; a Prophet is a force behind the vision. These have the foresight to see the invisible. They can visualize the apostle's ideas and interpret them into predictions and workable theories. Every step needed to bring the vision to fruition must be sanctioned and often predicted by the prophets. Otherwise, success may be unattainable.

The prophets are those with foresight into the future. They may do this either by patterns or insights. They see what others do not see or may ignore. This gift can be found and fueled by physical things (such as numbers, patterns, experiences, instincts etc.) and the spiritual (receiving explicit instruction from the almighty God or going into business with the devil). These have eyes for patterns and seasons and can make almost accurate predictions of the future based on their giftings. Due to this fact, they are often called upon to make predictions. Therefore, apostles need prophets before venturing into any new idea.

There is a history professor called Allan Lichtman. He has developed the 13 key indicators; this has helped him to accurately predict the winner of every United States Presidential election since 1984. His prediction was accurate again in 2020. Such is a primary example of prophetic gifting in the kingship realm today. The 13 keys that he developed by observation have been there for all to see since the beginning of time, but only a prophet like him could see them and bring them together in such a way as to produce accurate predictions. Yes, it is way better to hear from God directly; but God, in His mercy, knows that some will never approach Him. So, He made it possible for some humans like Professor Lichtman to have such insight into the future based on history, patterns etc. Other examples of such are the economists who specialize in predicting the future. The meteorologists predict the weather, and the computer programmers design algorithms (that indicate what you might want next). Therefore, we see that any venture's success rate is based on its prophets' accurate prediction. They are the force behind the success of any idea. When their prediction goes wrong, it can cause significant losses. For example, when Target ventured into Canada, it ended up in losses. Perhaps this happened because of the errors of their prophets. Thus, before an organization ventures into any idea, they send people with these gifts (Prophets) out to study (often called feasibility study) and make predictions.

As per Amos 3:7, *Surely the Lord GOD does nothing, Unless He reveals His secret to His servants the prophets.* Since this is the domain of humans (Genesis 1:26), God must tell someone in this realm before God can do anything in this realm. Then this individual turns and makes predictions based on what God has revealed. Such is God's intention for Prophets and how He related with everyone in His sphere. Simply put, the work of a prophet will be more accurate in the kingship or priesthood realm if they allow God to drive this gift. For example, in the kingship, God can tell you what to look for and the results. He can guide your path to the correct information and research. And for those in the Priesthood, this He does primarily through dreams, visions, citing Biblical references, etc. We see that regardless of our realm, the prophetic is only as good as the information a person possesses. God may not talk to or show an individual beyond their knowledge (John 14:26). In this same way, predictions are made based on the knowledge possessed or acquired. However, searching for this information and knowledge can be easy (with God) or extremely tedious (without God).

No matter how easy we think getting that information is, it would be easier with God. So let us examine it from this view, the gift itself was given to us by God through Jesus. It means that if we are to get the best out of it, supplementing it with God is the best way.

Prophets are naturally attracted to information. Their giftings can pull information, so they are knowledge seekers. They are, therefore, studious and like research. This way, they are armed with the knowledge to make the correct predictions. There are many titles they may hold in the kingship sphere, but as the Priesthood is concerned, these are prophets.

Weakness

There are many weaknesses associated with this office. But for the sake of our study here, we will highlight pride.

Pride

As mentioned earlier, the prophets possess information; they are studious and, as such, can be highly intelligent. Due to this fact, if care is not taken, their possessions, intelligence, and foresight can make them condescend (a form of pride). They may look at others as dumb or just plain stupid. A prophet must remember that this gift is from God, and as such only humility can keep it afloat (James 4:6). We must also remember that the gift is not for us. Because it is God's, the increase of this gift is based on Him because He *resists the proud but gives grace to the humble.* (James 4:6). Like Samson, we can lose any gift of God if we do not follow His prescriptions. Others who are not in this office may never see what you see. We must understand this and have compassion. We must be empathic enough to go to the extra length to make our predictions relatable and understanding. What benefit are such predictions if others (especially those implementing them) can't make sense of it? Do not write people off just because they are not in your office or getting it. This attitude is the highway to reducing and losing this gift of Christ.

The Evangelists

Now that we have established the generic and relatable definitions and attributes of the Apostles and Prophets, it is time to discuss the next logical one—The Evangelists. It is incredible that this also comes next, even in the scriptural order. Think about it; the Apostle pioneered the vision; the plans, strategies, and predictions have been drawn out by the prophets in conjunction with the Apostles. So, the next logical thing to do is to start spreading the news about what is about to come or new. So this, therefore, brings us to the Evangelists. In the kingship realm, this department is often known as sales, promotions, marketing etc. So, once an idea is conceptualized in the C-suite, it goes through the various stages of the Prophetic for strategies and actualization. After this, the sales department takes this and spreads it. Otherwise, it will yield no benefit to the organization. It makes the evangelist a significant asset to any company, including the body of Christ. These critical fellows are the ones we are about to discuss.

Let's define the evangelists generically as we have done with the first two offices. Once again, we see a great definition from Google: an evangelist is a zealous advocate of something. Once an idea is birthed, these are the ones who tend to advocate the idea to others. They do this with their un-rival ability to persuade others to buy into the idea. So, we see the word zealous used to describe them. In addition, as defined by google, this word implies that evangelists can display great energy and enthusiasm in pursuing a cause or objective. Therefore, evangelists can be very energetic, excited, and elated about a thing they are passionate about. All this is naturally domiciled in the evangelist's office.

As per 1 John 1:1, the evangelists are especially more effective, excited, energetic, and elated about what they have touched and handled. That is, things that they know, understand, and have experienced. Therefore, they must be brought up to speed on the matter.

The evangelists are the front-line workers and sellers of the idea. They are the ones that every other person outside of the organization will encounter first. If the idea is going to survive or die, it solely rests on the abilities of the evangelists. They are the first impression and the most important for new ideas reaching the intended customers. Regardless of the work done by the other offices, if an evangelist fails in their responsibilities, all the effort will be futile. In this way, any organization with this office is bound to succeed and excel in reaching the intended customers. Therefore, Jesus reinforced the significance of this office when *He said to them, "Go into all the world and preach the gospel to every creature* (Mark 16:15).

Weaknesses

Though this office has many weaknesses, we will focus on two main flaws: exaggeration and depreciation/loss of zeal.

Exaggeration

Exaggeration is simply a misrepresentation of the fact. Due to this office's zeal, energy and enthusiasm, an evangelist must especially look out for exaggeration. In their quest to spread the news and let everyone know how incredible the vision they have caught is, an evangelist may add and subtract from the fact. They may do this knowingly or unknowingly. Exaggeration is simply a fancy word for *lying*. It is an act of recounting things in a way that is not true or entirely true. We see this example during the fall of man in Genesis 3. This act is simply deception, and God will not stand for it. As we saw in Genesis 3, when the devil engaged in this, it brought curses. Therefore, when we engage in exaggeration, we make ourselves candidates for curse(s).

There is already a perception of this for those in this office. But this doesn't in any way mean that we must follow suit. So, an evangelist must especially be watchful and present nothing but the truth. The gift of the evangelist does not need help by lying to be effective. If we rely on the Holy Spirit, we can make this gift highly effective with the truth. Jesus commanded us in Matthew 5:37 to let our yes be yes, and our no be no. And as per Revelations 21:8, all liars are destined for hell. No noble cause on earth, including salvation, justifies exaggeration. It only leads us on the path of death (Proverbs 14:12).

Here is the fact, as we have discussed, the gift of the evangelist is a gift from Christ (Ephesians 4:8). Since God is the God of truth (Deuteronomy 32:4), His gifts are only highly effective when it is engaged with the truth. If an evangelist presents what they like and why they like it, this gifting has its way of being highly effective. Exaggerations become needed when the evangelist does not believe in what they are selling. Before we sign up to use this gift for anything, we should ensure that we are into the idea. We must learn to ask all the questions that will get us excited about it. Learn to build the zeal. Exaggeration is a natural filler for zeal. If we are not zealous about an idea, we must lie to sell that idea. Only truth can bring out the best of the evangelist. It is when the gift truly works as design.

Depreciation/Loss of zeal

As we have discussed in the first weakness, the zeal of an evangelist is connected to their knowledge of an idea. Therefore, when an evangelist loses their passion, they lack some knowledge. Often, the knowledge they are trading with is old information. So, an evangelist must always have the latest and greatest information to keep their zeal going. For example, in Christendom, most evangelists do not get tired of sharing about God. Why? They keep learning and seeing the new manifestation of God in their life and ministry; this becomes a revelation—new knowledge that keeps their zeal on fire. Any evangelist without such brand-new insight and current knowledge can quickly lose their zeal.

Due to this fact, evangelists must strive always to get this information. Though they are not naturally built to research and read, they can and should buddy up with someone who can deduce new revelations. Therefore, an evangelist should have at least a teacher in their orbit. The streams of the teaching office can keep the evangelist wet, thereby always keeping their zeal.

The Pastors

The word Pastor seems very strictly restricted to the Christian sects. Thus, it may be almost impossible to find the meaning of a Pastor from a secular—kingship perspective. But as we have learnt and established, there is a variation of every priestly office in the kingship realm. A Pastor is no different. Therefore, since almost all known definitions are from the Priestly perspective, we will use these definitions to understand the variation in the kingship realm.

As per Google, a pastor is a minister in charge of a Christian church or congregation. A definition like this relates to the priesthood. Since a minister in this context is simply a person working in a unique capacity, we will replace a minister with a person. As such, the definition becomes a person in charge of a congregation. Looking into the meaning of congregation, as per Google, we see this is simply a gathering or collection of people, animals, or things. Therefore, a pastor is responsible for a group of people, animals, or things. From here, there may be various definitions for this role, but if you are in charge of a collection of people, things, and animals, you are in this fantastic office.

Putting this back into the office's puzzle, we will understand why this comes right after the evangelists. The moment the evangelist campaigns are yielding results, Pastors are needed. Their role is to manage the results of the campaign's success. They are to look after, care for and manage the collection of people, animals, or things they are in charge of. What they care for will depend on the target of the idea and the result of the evangelist campaign. Such makes them the most important in sustaining the idea. For example, an apostle comes up with an idea—partners with prophets who can strategize, predict, and produce a prototype. The evangelist picks up the train and blasts it to the world. Business begins to roll, and now managers of all kinds (Admin Manager, Financial Manager, Human

Resource Manager, Project Manager, etc.) are needed. All these kinds of Managers are variations of this office. Due to the domiciled caring ability in this office, we see a variation in this also in nurses, doctors, and many medical personnel.

Anyone who cares about what they have been charged with operates in the Pastoral realm. We must have heard of a group that worked together, and they saw each other as family. The head of this group is a true pastor. A pastor's gift helps bind the flock together with love as a natural family bond. Therefore, Pastoral grace is fatherly. The trademark of this office is LOVE. Jesus said in John 10:11 that He is the good shepherd (Pastor). So, He died for humanity. Anyone in this office operates in this kind of love mainly for who or what they've been charged. Such love is something that other offices may not fully grasp.

We see that though in the Priesthood realm, they are known as Pastors, in the Kingship realm, their title is endless. The role they play is what places them in the office.

Weakness

The only weakness of this office we will discuss here is the only thing that sets this office apart: Love.

Love

The last thing on the fruit of the Spirit list in Galatians 5:22-23 was self-control. And as per Proverbs 25:28, *Whoever has no rule over his own spirit is like a city broken down, without walls.* Pastors are prone to loving others more than themselves. From Jesus' instruction in Mark 12:30-31, this is a sin. We are to love our neighbour as ourselves. So, genuine love for others is possible when we truly love God first, above all, and then ourselves and others. Due to a Pastor's caring ability, they may experience burnout and even die early. Those in this office must understand that God has called them to manage specific people and not to be their God. Only God can love every single individual totally and absolutely. You must locate and recognize the people you are sent to, your neighbours (See Luke 10:25-37), and love them accordingly. That is, in the same proportion as you love yourself. Therefore, a Pastor's effectiveness is based on their love for themselves. Another point here is that though a Pastor might feel like they ought to love every individual on the face of the earth, their primary love obligation is to those they have been charged.

Hear this, only love well spent can yield good results. You will only get good results from your love seed if planted in the right soil, i.e. the right people. We ought to love everybody but not invest love into everybody. Such is a weakness that the devil will explore; this massive gap leaves a Pastor vulnerable and killable. Therefore, self-control and self-discipline are a must for this office. All pastors must develop these two essentials before operating in this office; otherwise, offences, disappointment, discouragement and burnout are just around the corner. To learn more about discipline, please read A Disciplined Life by Emmanuel Adewusi and Boundaries by Dr. Henry Cloud and Dr. John Townsend.

The Teachers

Many may assume that since this office was listed last, it must be less critical. Such an assumption is not just wrong; it can hinder a person from benefiting from the office. Like every other office, this is needed and essential. However, the importance of this office has made it a target for the devil. He has made people despise this office because any knowledge worth having will come through this office. Now whatever you despise will never work for you. The devil thrives in darkness, so he can easily steal, kill, and destroy when people don't know (Hosea 4:6). The teacher is, therefore, a major enemy of the devil. It is the same reason people lack knowledge but won't ask questions. Ignorance is not bliss; it is deadly. Such is the reason why this office is critical. It is the only office in the body of Christ whose title is not generally used. Nobody introduces themselves as a Teacher the same way other offices say I am Pastor, Prophet, Apostle, or Evangelist. Such signifies the devil's unfortunate success in despising the teacher's office.

Dictionary.com defines a teacher as an individual who teaches or instructs, especially as a professional or instructor. As per Google, to teach is to show or explain to (someone) how to do something. Substituting this into the definition, a teacher is, therefore, an individual who shows or explains to someone how to do something. Thus, without this office, the practicality of an idea to others becomes lost, and the idea will not survive beyond the initial set of people.

From the definition above, we see that the sustainability of any idea lies in the ability to teach it to others. This Jesus understood and thereby gave the gift of teachers. Many great ideas have been lost due to the need for better teachers. Therefore, the laws derived in science and many other fields are still in effect and well understood today because they have been passed down from generation to generation through the help of teachers. Jesus spent most of His approximately three years of ministry teaching more than anything else. He was called Rabbi, which means teacher in different places in the Bible. Then with what we can deem as the equivalent of His dying breath, He charged His disciples to teach others what He had taught them (Matthew 28:20). This shows the importance of this office even to Jesus. Thus, it doesn't matter how much God has shown us; it only produces results beyond us when we teach them to others. It is often said that there is no success without a successor. The teaching office ensures a successor is made. Many spiritual concepts, ideas and principles are lost today simply because the teachers of the old failed. There is a lot in God, but posterity doesn't need to reinvent the wheel. They can start from where the primogenitor stops. But when teachers of old fail to teach, then wheels will have to be reinvented.

Sadly, in Christendom, it is as if God starts with each generation from the beginning. We must understand that growth is based on a sequence of information. Therefore, *precept must be upon precept, precept upon precept, line upon line, line upon line, here a little, there a little.* (Isaiah 28:10). One thing must be known for another to be shown and for us to benefit from it. When the foundation is not laid, then the work must start from the beginning. But imagine if we have the foundation laid, the growth will move faster (Haggai 2:9).

To put this in perspective, by the grace of God, I plan to empty everything God has taught me before I leave this earth. As such, anyone who picks up on that and reads everything I wrote or written about me and all my teachings will start their journey from where I stopped. They will move to the next phase of things I could not, and they will progress even faster.

The office of a teacher, like every other office, is universal. It is applicable in the kingship and the Priesthood. They are needed and essential in the secular world and the spiritual world. So, at some point in life, everyone had someone who showed them how to do something. We are what we are and do what we do the way we do it because someone taught us. Life is all about lessons; this means there are people teaching us something every day. Either actively or passively. Such makes this office extremely important.

One thing that sets this office apart is its ability to articulate and teach something in a way its audience can grasp. We know there is a difference between having an idea and being able to articulate it and teach it to others. The office of a teacher can adjust based on the student. Individuals in this office can go to any length as needed to get the correct information for teaching. They are wired to research, that is, search out the truth and present it in the simplest way to help their audience understand. This gift directs them to all kinds of information; they are prone to information that may help them and others. They are the core of any idea that must survive. Without teaching, great things, like concepts, principles, and ideas, may be lost forever.

Lastly, on a particular subject, a teacher is expected to have "all" the answers pertaining to what they are teaching. Though this may seem unrealistic, it is still a general expectation for a teacher. They are highly knowledgeable as it pertains to their specialty. For example, in Matthew 5, 6 and 7, we saw Jesus, who happens to be the most outstanding teacher of all, teach on different topics as it pertains to spirituality; why? Because that was His specialty. Therefore, to benefit from this gift, we must put "pressure" on its carrier, that is, ask questions as they pertain to the calling and specialty of the individual teachers. As we do this, the gift in that person, if genuine, must answer us. By the grace of God, you may never hear the word "I don't know" from a genuine God-ordained teacher as it pertains to their specialty. Such is because the Holy Spirit within them works with their giftings to give the correct answer as always needed.

Weakness

For the sake of our studies, we will highlight only two weaknesses of the teaching office: pride and deception.

There are two distinct ways that pride can manifest in this office. First, when the estimation of our self-importance is not aligned with what it is in reality, it is pride. Therefore, the first form of pride is overestimating our importance, and the second is underestimating our importance (low self-esteem). Consequently, we will take them one at a time to dilate further.

Pride—to overestimate one's importance

Pride can also manifest as being critical of others, especially when they happen to be talking/teaching about our specialty. Due to the nature of this office, it is easy to think that they are the only one that knows it all, specifically in the area where God has given us grace and insights. With this mindset, such individuals forget that the original idea and the platform may have come from another, that is, the Apostle and others who made the idea worth learning and teaching. For example, without the evangelist's work, the teacher may have no one to teach. Such is pride in the office of a teacher. A teacher must understand that any successful adventure is a product of a team of individuals. As such, we are not the only ones with grace for what we do. This demonic tool can be thwarted when teachers surround themselves with other offices. Humble themselves to be under the authority God has set for us. It will help to see how all the puzzle pieces fit together. The great Apostle Paul, who happens to be one of the greatest teachers after Jesus in the New Testament, was subject to the Apostles in Jerusalem, as seen in Acts 21:23-27. A teacher must learn to be under authority. Because the teaching office is only one piece of the overarching theme, the authority that God has set in place is equipped to see the big picture; as such, they can steer us right. Based on their sights and foresight, it is the job of the authority to help us see and estimate ourselves in the right light. Despite the wealth of information, revelation, and grace a teacher carries, they must be in the company of other offices and be under authority (the word, the Holy Spirit and human authority) as ordained by God. It is the solution to any form of pride in this office.

Pride—To underestimate one's importance

Due to the devil's success in despising this office, a teacher may find themselves swimming against the current in some settings. It is the ocean where teachers are despised, not recognized, or accepted. If this is the case, a teacher must employ the command of Jesus in Matthew 10:14 (*And whoever will not receive you nor hear your words, when you depart from that house or city, shake off the dust from your feet*). The teaching office fulfills its purpose and is truly beneficial when a teachable spirit meets it. Otherwise, a teacher stands a risk of despising their gifts and hence low self-esteem. We have not been called to everyone, and those that chose not to listen may not be ripe for the information or are not our responsibilities. Also, the fact that we know something doesn't mean we need to share it. There is time for everything (Ecclesiastes 3); when the right thing is done at the wrong time, it is still wrong, and the result will be as such. A teacher must be around those to whom they have been called. It is here that the teaching grace truly thrives. As mentioned earlier, a teacher is appropriately utilized and given the proper estimate in the right light by being under the correct authority ordained by God.

Deception

The office of a teacher is an office responsible for demystifying information. As such, a teacher must study, research, and prove all things and hold on to what is truth (1 Thessalonians 5:21). They are expected to do this at a larger scale to ensure copacetic delivery. In any setting, be it natural or spiritual, it is the responsibility of the teacher to communicate the most difficult things in the easiest way that we can understand. Many in the other offices know things but may need help sharing them with others. But the teachers are gifted with the ability to understand and communicate with others; they are equipped with the necessary flexibility to aid the student learning. So, many will rely on the words and teachings of a teacher. They will ask questions and take the answers and teaching of a teacher as the holy grail on the subject. As such, the teachers are targets for the devil. If the devil could deceive a teacher and feed them lies, many would be bound by the same lies. So, teachers must do their research with such understanding and responsibility. From James 3:1 (*My brethren, let not many of you become teachers, knowing that we shall receive a stricter judgment*), we see that God has a higher baseline for teachers. If we are called into this office, we are called into responsibilities. It is our job to ensure that what we are presenting to others is the truth from God and not from our feelings, emotions and experience. We must have a system to check every insight and revelation we get. In the priesthood, a teacher must always check everything on the scale of the written word.

Anything that we cannot find directly or indirectly from the written word—aka the Bible must not be taught as the truth. Also, teachers in this realm must understand the difference between doctrines and non-doctrines. Yes, *all Scripture is given by inspiration of God and is profitable for doctrine, for reproof, for correction, for instruction in righteousness, that the man of God may be complete, thoroughly equipped for every good work* (2 Timothy 3:16-17). However, we must understand that some are written to give us some information in our quest to know God better. As per Deuteronomy 19:15, *one witness shall not rise against a man concerning any iniquity or any sin that he commits; by the mouth of two or three witnesses, the matter shall be established.*

In the same way, *one witness shall not rise to affirm anything as a doctrine; by the witness of two or three witnesses, the matter shall be established as doctrine.* So, before we teach anything from the written word as doctrine, a teacher must look for more than one witness from the written word specifically. Otherwise, such are non-doctrinal; this I called *for your information* only. So, in the priestly realm, the written word, with the help of the inner witness of the Holy Spirit, is the primary validator of a teacher's insight to escape deception. Please read Protection from Deception by Derek Prince for more information and learning.

Putting it all together

In summary, Jesus died for all men, and He gave gifts to all humankind (2 Corinthians 5:15 & Ephesians 4:8). As such, there is one or more of these gifts in every human (saved or unsaved) alive. Due to this fact, wherever humans gather, we will see all these gifts on display. Yes, it is possible to learn skills from other offices, but we should learn what will help us advance in our gifting. For example, if an evangelist is asked something beyond "selling," they might have difficulty communicating the truth. It is not necessarily because they are bad at their job but because they might not understand yet or lack specific communication skills. So, such individuals must sit and learn from a teacher, where communicating the truth in the simplest form is innate.

Also, these offices are given by Jesus to make the overarching goal achievable. Each office is not designed to stand alone but to fuse to achieve the common goal. Therefore, in every congregation, different people assume unassigned positions. The secular world has called them leaders and followers. But in fact, these are the five offices that individuals assume.

These offices are emphasized in Christendom so that we can achieve the aim of the body of Christ. When Jesus was leaving the earth, He left the mission's survival mainly in the Apostles' hands. The leader determines if any assignment is to survive or fail.

The Apostles see the total vision; these are the visionaries. They know how every part of the vision fits into one another. Once the Apostles have enough vision in their sight, the only other office that can see what they see and put it in perspective are the prophets. The prophets are gifted at fine-tuning crazy ideas into relatable ones. They see things from a different perspective. They see the outcomes and provide solutions to those problems. *A prophet who sees doom without a solution is not worthy of office.* The same gifting that shows destruction can give answers. Now that we have the vision and the achievable goal insight, we want to get the results out there. Next is the evangelist, who takes the idea and blows it up. They spread it like wildfire with energy and passion to anyone who cares to listen. They are naturally talented to get in your face and sell you what you may never have wanted in the first place. They are wired to seem more excited and invested in the idea than the other office. They are the most energetic of all. As people come in and get involved, the company grows more prominent. As we grow bigger, we require managers and leaders; these are the Pastors. They take care of the people who are getting involved. They are caring, loving and kind in all they do. They are prone to put other people's issues over their own. They are the most affectionate of all. They operate in such love that might be incomprehensible to other offices. Unfortunately, the devil can also explore the strength of this office to bring the individuals in this office down. Finally, if the integrity of the ideal is to remain, then it must be taught correctly and consistently. Information missed or omitted can cause the vision to be incomplete. It is here where the ones gifted to present information in its entirety and as simple without omitting anything are brought in. These are the teachers. Therefore, anything that wasn't carried forward from previous generations is simply an indication of failed teachers of the times. What posterity lacks are simply the lapses of progenitor teachers.

In this way, we see that any idea's accomplishment and sustainability rest on each office's shoulders. With the Apostles at the helm of leadership, the offices work hand in hand to achieve the goal set before them.

Chapter 2

Find Yourself

In the previous chapter, we explored the options and streams available to everyone. However, we must understand that though these are the available streams and options, these can only produce results when we locate ourselves and start putting in the necessary work. Therefore, in this chapter, we will explore practical steps to discover ourselves and ensure that we always align with God's intention for our creation.

Before we continue, many might say why do I have to use the gift? We will see and analyze this question and other things that will enhance our understanding from the parable of Jesus in Matthew 25:14-30.

"For the kingdom of heaven is like a man traveling to a far country, who called his own servants and delivered his goods to them. And to one he gave five talents, to another two, and to another one, to each according to his own ability; and immediately he went on a journey. Then he who had received the five talents went and traded with them and made another five talents. And likewise, he who had received two gained *two more also. But he who had received one went and dug in the ground and hid his lord's money. After a long time, the lord of those servants came and settled accounts with them. "So, he who had received five talents came and brought five other talents, saying, 'Lord, you delivered to me five talents; look, I have gained five more talents besides them.' His lord said to him, 'Well done, good and faithful servant; you were faithful over a few things I will make you ruler over many things. Enter into the joy of your lord.' He also who had received two talents came and said, 'Lord, you delivered to me two talents; look, I have gained two more talents besides them.' His lord said to him, 'Well done, good and faithful servant; you have been faithful over a few things, I will make you ruler over many things. Enter into joy of your lord.' "Then he who had received the one talent came and said, 'Lord, I knew you to be a hard man, reaping where you have not sown, and gathering where you have not scattered seed. And I was afraid and went and hid your talent in the ground. Look, there you have what is yours.' "But his lord answered and said to him, 'wicked and lazy servant, you knew that I reap where I have not sown and gather where I have not scattered seed. So, you ought to have deposited my money with the bankers, and at my coming I would have received back my own with interest. Therefore, take the talent from him and give it to him who has ten talents. For to everyone who has, more will be given, and he will have abundance; but from him who does not have, even what he has will be taken away. And cast the unprofitable servant into the outer darkness. There will be weeping and gnashing of teeth.'*

The Scripture above was a parable by Jesus about how things work in heaven's kingdom. But this He did in a very familiar term. For our studies, the man in this parable is God. He made us and gave us talents and giftings that put us in different offices based on our abilities. From the scriptures, we saw a servant with five and another with two and one.

In the same way, some among us today may find themselves in multiple offices while others might be in one. Such is not an indication of superiority but rather what each one of us can handle now based on our composition (Ephesians 4:7). But here is something interesting; the servants with more than one gift got to work and produced double the talent results while the servant with one gift did nothing. The phenomenon is still valid as the one with multiple abilities seems to have results. In contrast, others tend to wallow in self-pity heaped on them by the devil.

As we have discussed in Chapter 1, this discussion applies to all believers and non-believers. Also, no matter what we think we know of our calling, vision, and missions, these are mini destinies for the time being; there is always more, even within one office. Therefore, we need to produce and make the best use of what we have and know now, and the next phase will open. For example, If the servant with one had traded with it and gained one more, they would automatically move from one talent to two—increased capacity. Therefore, your way to more talents lies in the one you currently have. Therefore, engage what you currently have, and it will transport you to the top you desire. But the devil is a master of stagnation and lies. Since he can't stop God from giving us a gift(s), he stops us from producing and moving to the next phase.

Lastly, since we were given these gifts, we must understand that the giver will come back at the appointed time not necessarily known to us to settle the accounts

(Revelations 22:12). Whenever this time is, we must be ready because every visit of the master is a potential change of level for good or bad. Yes, heaven is the ultimate, but as we see from these scriptures, He will check in here on earth now and then.

In the next portion of the scriptures above, we saw the acceptable results—It is double or nothing. The servant with five was required to produce five more, and so on. Therefore, *to whom much is given, from him much will be required; and to whom much has been committed, of him they will ask the more* (Luke 12:48).

I must reiterate from these scriptures the master gave the talent to each servant based on their ability. It has nothing to do with loving one more than the other. No, He is a good master who understood the capacity of each servant and gave them work accordingly. So, in the same way, each of us was given gifts and required to produce results synonymous with what we have been given. Therefore, as we produce these results, we are also required to trade with the new results and produce even more and on and on it goes. Such was reflected in Amos 6:1 (*Woe to you who are at ease in Zion*). Until our death, there is no "ease." We are required to keep on trading and making profits with the gifting we have and those we've gained. For example, five are needed to produce five more. When the master comes to settle the account, the five is added, meaning that the next time the master comes, this servant will be required to produce twenty, and on it goes. Such is a typical application to Tom Sachs' quote: "the reward for good work is more work." May God help us.

We will conclude our analysis on this note. Those that traded with what was given, in addition to increased capacity, will gain the praise of the master; and have access to what they needed to bring about more results. But those not using theirs stand the risk of losing even what they currently have. Such is the fastest way to penury and miserable life. Therefore, we must find ourselves and start utilizing what we have. Hence the necessity of this chapter.

Who Are You?

Many of us have asked ourselves a question like this once or a few times already. This kind of question is what we will call an existential question. It speaks to the reason why we exist. There are two ways we can find a satisfying answer to this question. But one is better than the other. One guarantees a response with less stress and guessing in that it puts the responsibility on another. In contrast, the second puts the responsibility on us. So we will dig deep into the best way and briefly touch the other way.

Here is a simple fact: it makes no sense when we are looking for the answer to such questions as this not to consult our creator. Therefore, the best way is the *way of the creator*, while the other way is the *way of the creation*. For example, if I want to know about a car, the best way is to look at the car manufacturer or what they have provided, such as manuals. Yes, I might get some insight by studying the car and learning. But this could take time and cost me, such as learning from my errors.

Option One: The Way of the Creator

The first option we will explore is the *best*, and that is "the way of the creator." This way, as said earlier, directly puts the responsibility of an answer on the creator. For better analysis, we can all agree that humans did not just appear from thin air. Even a newborn was born with an unprecedented number of consistencies and perfection in design. Looking at the complexity of the human body, the orderliness, the perfect synergy and many more, the human body was made to function that way. Therefore, we know something is off when a part doesn't function as designed. But who designed the body to operate this way? We seek to uncover this Being in a genuine and practical way. Once this is done, we will see how to approach this Being that made us with this existential question. Though we are different, as evident in our fingerprints, the method discussed here is a universal way to locate and approach our maker to deduce our destiny.

The Maker of Humanity

The maker of humans is the one who made humans. Many might think that since babies are conceived through the coming together of a man and a woman, they made the baby. Such a notion is not just wrong but doesn't make sense. Let's think about it if that is the case, how is it that not all sex ends up in pregnancy? Yes, the baby knitting together starts with the man and woman coming together, but this does not make them the maker. For example, when you order a Tesla online, the process of making that car is set in motion. That doesn't mean that you made the Tesla vehicle.

In the same way, someone else made us and knitted us together in our mother's womb. It is this Entity we want to uncover. All things being equal, by the time a newborn arrives on earth, we can all see and tell that an Entity has spent time on the perfection of every detail of the baby's design, both internally and externally.

In Genesis 2:7 (*And the LORD God formed man of the dust of the ground and breathed into his nostrils the breath of life; and man became a living being.*), we saw the beginning of the first man Adam. So, from here, we see that the Lord God created the first man. In the same vein, Genesis 2:21 (*And the LORD God caused a deep sleep to fall on Adam, and he slept; and He took one of his ribs and closed the flesh in its place. Then the rib which the LORD God had taken from man He made into a woman, and He brought her to the man.*), we saw the first woman was created, and again her creator was the Lord God. From here, we can deduce that the origin of man starts with the Lord God. He started it; therefore, He puts man and woman in motion. But Adam and Eve were never conceived. So, who made everyone conceived after Adam and Eve? We find the answer to this in Psalm 139:13 and Isaiah 44:24. Let us take each scripture and see the common denominator.

You made all the delicate, inner parts of my body and knit me together in my mother's womb. Psalm 139:13 NLT

From Psalm 139:1, David was talking about the Lord when He made the statement in the scripture above. So, from here, we see that the Lord was and is still responsible for making man through the womb even today.

Thus says the LORD, your Redeemer, And He who formed you from the womb: "I am the LORD, who makes all things, who stretches out the heavens all alone, who spreads abroad the earth by Myself; Isaiah 44:24.

Like David, we saw the prophet Isaiah affirm that we were formed in the womb by our maker, the Lord.

Bringing it all together, we see that the Lord God made the first people. After this, all-subsequent humans were knitted together in the womb by the hands of the Lord. So, the first model was made by the Lord and God (The Lord God), while the Lord made the subsequent models.

The Lord God Vs the Lord

From our explanation above, we have established the creator and maker is Lord God and Lord. Therefore, in this subsection, we will explore these two.

The grace of the Lord Jesus Christ, and the love of God, and the communion of the Holy Spirit be with you all. Amen. 2 Corinthians 13:14

From the scripture above, we can deduce that three personalities are mentioned here—Lord Jesus Christ, God, and the Holy Spirit. These three are what we understand in Christendom as the trinity. It means that the God we serve chose to reveal Himself to us in three forms-as the Father-God, the Son-Jesus, and the Holy Spirit. Though they may operate as separate Beings with different responsibilities, these three are still ONE! (Deuteronomy 6:4 & Mark 12:29). To learn more about this concept, I implore you to read my books "The Person You Should Know and The Most Important Person of Our Time."

As per the scriptures, Jesus is Lord (Romans 10:9, 1 Corinthians 12:3 & 2 Corinthians 4:5). So, the maker from our deduction is Jesus and God. Applying this to our previous explanations, we see that the creation of the first people was the Lord (Jesus) God, that is, the conjunction of God and Jesus (Genesis 2:7 & 21), while the Lord Jesus put together the subsequent humans (Psalm 139:13 & Isaiah 44:24).

But why are the Lord and God involved like this? We see the answer to this in 1 Corinthians 12:4-6.

There are diversities of gifts, but the same Spirit. There are differences of ministries, but the same Lord. And there are diversities of activities, but it is the same God who works all in all.

From 1 Corinthians 14:33, we know God is a God of order. He hates chaos. As such, God ensures that we all have our places and responsibilities. He hates waste and doesn't like being idle. Therefore, if you are alive today, you have a place and responsibilities here on earth. It is the same way for the Trinity. All have unique responsibilities within the Trinity, from God to Jesus and the Holy Spirit. The scripture above opens our eyes to one of their many responsibilities. From here, we see that the Holy Spirit distributes the gifts while Jesus administers and allocates services and ministries. On the other hand, God determines the works and activities.

To help us understand, let us take car manufacturing as an example. The design team came up with an idea. After which, they work with the manufacturing team to create a prototype. Once this is done and tested, they leave the design blueprint and manufacturing to the manufacturing team. This team may now deduce an easier way to ease mass production. In this very similar way is the making of humans. God determined that He wanted to make humans; from Genesis 1:26, we understand that He already had a design in mind. So, it was God, not the Lord God, that said, "*let us make man in our image.*" Such is the work; however, this work will require ministry, administration and services to make this happen. This work is, therefore, Jesus' responsibility. Therefore, the Lord God, that is the Lord "&" God created the first human together. However, after the success of the first "prototype" (Adam and Eve), the mass production of the subsequent human was left in the hand of the Lord (Jesus). Now He has a blueprint and knows how the first was successfully made. God and Jesus already ironed out the plan to make more humans. But it was left in the hands of the service unit (manufacturing) to produce more humans in different shapes and sizes. Therefore, *all things were made through Him (Jesus), and without Him (Jesus) nothing was made that was made.* John 1:3, emphasis mine.

So, all things, including humans, were made through Jesus (Colossians 1:16). From the first people till today and forever, man's making through pregnancy is the work of the Lord Jesus, who knit us together in the womb. He is the nature behind conception, pregnancy, and delivery. Thus, when it comes to humans, Jesus is our only ally. He knows us through and through (Hebrews 4:15). Therefore, Jesus stepped in to be our savior when we were in trouble. *Thus, no salvation in any other, for there is no other name under heaven given among men by which we must be saved."* (Acts 4:12). It is only the one that made us that can save us. Similarly, our best option is Jesus any day when we find ourselves in trouble.

Since Jesus and God were involved, do we have two makers? The simple answer is no. The one who designs is the maker. He is the creator. However, using the car company example again, the designer and the manufacturing team work for the same company. So, the company owns the right to the design and is the maker. In fact, in most cases, we have yet to find the name of the individual that came up with our car design.

In the same way, we can look at God, Jesus, and the Holy Spirit as such. They are members of the Trinity, so our maker is the Trinity. The enveloping and generic name for the Trinity is God. Thus, our maker is God. And God is the original designer; this makes Him the creator. We arrived at this same conclusion if we look at John 10:30, where Jesus said He and God (the Father) are one. It was confirmed in Mark 12:29 and Deuteronomy 6:4. As such, our maker from this analysis again is God. So, God is the maker and the creator. But we only get to know Him through our only ally and manufacturer-Jesus.

Getting to Know the Maker

We have established that God is our maker. God continues to make humans through Jesus. Thus, Jesus is the only connection between God and humans (1 Timothy 2:5). When it comes to humanity and God, the first and only stop is Jesus. There is no other link between humans and God except through Jesus. Because no other being was involved in the creation of humans except God, the Lord, and the creation—man and woman (See Genesis 2: 7 & 21), so, God looks to Jesus to connect with humans (John 3:16-18), and humans look to Jesus to connect with God (John 14:6). Consequently, if we are going to know our maker-God, we can only do so through Jesus.

I would like us to address a few questions here before we proceed. Jesus has earned His place as the mediator through His work on the cross. But do we need Him to know the maker? First off, as established, both Jesus and God are one. So, knowing Jesus is the same as knowing the Father (John 14:6 & 10-11). Secondly, a couple of things restrict us from approaching God directly. The first is our nature. God is holy (Leviticus 19:2 & 1 Peter 1:16); as such, He cannot even look at sin (Habakkuk 1:13). By virtue of the first people's sin, we are all sinners by nature (Romans 3:23 & 5:12). Therefore, David said *I was brought forth in iniquity, and in sin my mother conceived me* (Psalm 51:5). When explaining things to Moses in Exodus 33:20, God said: "*no one can see Him and live.*" God was saying that unless certain things are in place, encountering Him in our sinful nature can cause death (See 2 Samuel 6:7). Consequently, God has the children of Israel go through cleansing rituals before they can approach Him in time past. The second restriction is that God exists primarily in the spirit (John 4:24). But if we are alive here on earth, we primarily exist in the physical, though we are spirit beings. Unless we consciously activate our spirituality, we are earthly beings first. Therefore, we must be in the spirit to approach God (See Revelations 1:10).

Here is the dilemma in which we find ourselves. We need to get to God to get answers, but we can't. At least not in our current state. The good news is that God also wants us, and in John 3:16, He sent Jesus to solve these two issues. Jesus solves the first (our sinful nature) by being our substitute on the cross, forgiving our sins and creating a way to live without it in exchange for His righteousness (2 Corinthians 5:21). Once we subscribe to the Jesus program, we can *come boldly to the throne of grace, that we may obtain mercy and find grace to help in time of need* (Hebrews 4:16). Secondly, Jesus gave us access to the Holy Spirit who is the custodian of the realm of the Spirit in God (Acts 2:38). The Holy Spirit is the third Being of the Trinity, He connects us to the Spirit realm in God by *bearing witness with our spirit that we are children of God* (Romans 8:16). So, we see that through Jesus the barriers of restriction from getting to God are destroyed. Therefore, when Jesus died, *the veil of the temple was torn in two from top to bottom; and the earth quaked, and the rocks were split* (Matthew 27:51). This gave us the *boldness to enter the Holiest by the blood of Jesus* (Hebrews 10:19). To learn more about this extraordinary work of Jesus and the Holy Spirit, please read my book "The Most Important Person of Our Time and The Person You Should Know."

In summary, we can only get to God only through Jesus. We do this through the ways outlined in Romans 10:9-10.

...that if you confess with your mouth the Lord Jesus and believe in your heart that God has raised Him from the dead, you will be saved. For with the heart one believes unto righteousness, and with the mouth confession is made unto salvation.

It is the simple steps to subscribing to Jesus and gaining access to the God of all. All we must do is confess with our mouths that Jesus is Lord and believe in our earth that God has raised Him from the dead. As simple as this may sound, this is the only way. So, before we do this, we must understand that by confessing Jesus as Lord, we surrender to His Lordship. And by believing, we affirm that God can do the impossible and that Jesus died for our sins. Therefore, we have Jesus' righteousness (2 Corinthians 5:21), and old things are passed away (Romans 8:1). To do this, we must say the prayer below.

Dear Heavenly Father,

I come to you a sinner in need of a savior. I believe that Jesus died for my sins, and You raised Him from the dead. I confess Jesus as Lord and surrender to His Lordship. Thank you because now I know that I am saved, and I ask that you help me to remain and grow in You throughout my life. Amen

Ask the Maker

Prayer is the best and only way we talk to God about anything. The concept of prayer is a concept known to many. Christians do not just do it; many other religions also pray to their gods. However, if we are to pray to the God of all, there is a process to it that guarantees results. As I've alluded to, many religions do this, so doing this the right way is the only option to ensure we communicate with God. But before we explore this process, let us define prayer.

Prayer is simply a communication between God and humans. It can be in different forms. We can either engage in prayer to have a conversation with God (that is, prayer that requires an answer) (I Samuel 1), or we can relay information to God (that is, prayer that doesn't require a response) (See Psalm 142). After Jesus had called all His disciples, He did not teach them to preach, but He taught them to pray in Matthew 6:9-13. Apostle Paul in 1 Thessalonians 5:17 and Ephesians 6:18, practically advised us always to pray. These are indications of the importance of prayer.

A prayerless Christian cannot grow in God. They stand a chance of being swept away. Because we can only build relationships with those, we talk to. We lose touch with friendships and relationships with people when we don't talk to them. In the same way, if we don't talk to God often, we can lose our relationship with Him. The length of prayer is not a factor here, but rather the consistency and frequency of the communication. We grow in a relationship with a person we talk to for five minutes daily, more than the one we talk to for five hours every few weeks.

The Process

If I regard iniquity in my heart, The Lord will not hear. Psalm 66:18

God will not hear our prayer if we are in sin. However, as per Romans 3:23, all have sinned. You have sinned, I have sinned; every one of us has sinned. It means that none of us is qualified to pray to the Maker. It is here that Jesus stepped in to bridge this gap. Jesus is righteous and blameless (John 14:30). So, He can approach God. He came from God, and He and God are one (John 16:28 & John 10:30). Since righteousness is the only way to approach the Maker, Jesus gave us His righteousness and took our sin (1 Peter 2:24 & 2 Corinthians 5:21). So, now all we must do is to subscribe to this covering of Jesus following the prescription of Romans 10:9.

that if you confess with your mouth the Lord Jesus and believe in your heart that God has raised Him from the dead, you will be saved.

Once we do this, we can now use the righteous credit of Jesus to approach God (Hebrews 10:19 & Ephesians 3:12). *In that day, you will ask Me nothing. Most assuredly, I say to you, whatever you ask the Father in My name He will give you* (John 16:23). From this scripture, we understand that we are to approach God in the name of the one who redeemed us. Because He is our guarantor, we are now in Him (1 John

4:13). When we approach God, He sees His only begotten Son-Jesus. So, any prayer not prayed under this insurance of Jesus, and in His name, may not yield results.

The last part of the process is that since the realm of God is foreign to us, God has made it easy for us to pray the right things. Per 1 John 4:13 and Romans 8:14, the Spirit of God that comes to us through our subscription to Jesus' Insurance indicates that we are in God. As such, this same Spirit will help us pray or ask the right questions. *The Spirit also helps in our weaknesses. For we do not know what we should pray for as we ought, but the Spirit Himself makes intercession for us with groanings which cannot be uttered* (Romans 8:26).

In summary, we subscribe to the insurance of Jesus, as per Romans 10:9, and ask the Maker in the name of Jesus who redeemed us and whose credit we are using. We do this with the help of the Holy Spirit, the validator of our subscription (Ephesians 1:13 & Romans 8:9).

Receive an Answer

Let us start this section of our studies with this: God who made us with ears can hear, and He who made us with a mouth can speak (Psalm 94:9). If we can hear and reply, God can do even more. We must not be deceived. God speaks, and He hears. In the case of our studies in this book, the question we will be asking through prayer will require an answer. Thus, understanding how we get responses back from the Maker is critical. Many know how to ask but don't know how to receive answers. This section will look at practical ways to get replies back from God.

To expect an answer is to believe that God has heard us. It is confirmed in 1 John 5:14. *Now this is the confidence that we have in Him, that if we ask anything according to His will, He hears us.* So, our request must align with the will of God before we present it to God in prayer. If this is the case, then we know that God hears us (*Therefore, I say to you, whatever things you ask when you pray, believe that you receive them, and you will have them.* Mark 11:24). If He does, then we should expect an answer as needed. In our case, asking the Maker why we exist is a question that requires a response. It is the will of God because we are commanded to acknowledge God in all our ways (Proverbs 3:6). So, asking God about His plans for our life acknowledges Him as the Maker. God's desire is for us to come to Him for direction, then He can guide us. As we finish each mini destiny, we are to return to Him for more for as long as we live. Hence this is the best way.

Now how do we know it is time to stop praying and lean in for answers? There is something that Jesus said in John 16:24 *Until now you have asked nothing in My name. Ask, and you will receive, that your joy may be full.* Analyzing this scripture shows us one of the indicators that our prayer has been heard, and we can expect an answer. Until our joy is full, we have not received it. So, until our joy is full, we must continue praying like Daniel in Daniel 10. The prince of Persia withheld his answer for 21 days. He continued in prayer because his "joy was not full."

Joy is essential when dealing with God. In Isaiah 12:3, joy is needed to get anything from God. The blessing of salvation is activated when we approach with joy. Such is because the hallmark of our Maker-God is joy. Therefore, wherever

God is, there is joy Psalm 16:11. In Galatians 5:22-23, joy is the fruit of the Holy Spirit. As we have learnt, the Holy Spirit helps us to pray, and joy is a fruit of His. Therefore, when this joy becomes full, we know it is a signal from the Holy Spirit that the prayer has been heard. It is like ordering something online, and we wait for the notification. The fullness of joy is the notification from the Holy Spirit that our order has been processed and confirmed (Romans 8:16). In other words, we must pay attention to the one who helped us to pray to know if we have been heard.

As Christians, we must always be joyful (Philippians 4:4). Before prayer, joy is needed. But when our joy increases after a particular prayer point coupled with the feeling of satisfaction, this is an indication. So also, our joy is full when our joy is coupled with another fruit of the Spirit listed in Galatians 5:22-23 such as peace. At this point, we can enter God's rest and cease our prayers (Hebrews 4:10). We can lean in for answers.

The grace of the Lord Jesus Christ, and the love of God, and the communion of the Holy Spirit be with you all. Amen. 2 Corinthians 13:14

As we have alluded to, each Being of the Trinity has responsibilities. From the scripture above, we can see that communion is one of the Holy Spirit's. Therefore, to understand how we practically get answers from God, we must understand the communion ministry of the Holy Spirit.

Practical Step: Communion

Communion, as per Google, *is the sharing or exchanging of intimate thoughts and feelings, especially when the exchange is on a mental or spiritual level.* From this definition, we see that we need to be in communion with God if He is to share His thoughts with us. By praying, we have shared our thoughts with Him, and we should give Him a chance to share His. Remember, we pray with the help of the Holy Spirit, so there is a chance that we will hear back from God with His help as well. So, the Holy Spirit is the facilitator of communion with God. This work of the Holy Spirit is simply sharing or exchanging intimate thoughts between God and humans at a deeper level. As mentioned, we pray with the help of the Holy Spirit and receive answers primarily with the help of the Holy Spirit. Therefore, *God has revealed them to us through His Spirit. For the Spirit searches all things, yes, the deep things of God.* (1 Corinthians 2:10). To learn more about the ministry of the Holy Spirit in this dispensation, I encourage you again to read my book, "The Most Important Person of Our Time."

Let's drill even more resounding. In 1 Corinthians 2:11 NLT, the Bible shows us one of the intricacies of our nature and God's. It says *no one can know a person's thoughts except that person's own spirit, and no one can know God's thoughts except God's own Spirit.* So, from here, we know that the spirit of man is the custodian of the things of man and the Spirit of God, the Holy Spirit, is that of God. But according to Romans 8:16 NLT, we know that the Holy Spirit joins with our spirit. As such, our spirit is connected with the Holy Spirit. This connection is the point of contact between humans and God. It is here that the Holy Spirit helps us to pray the proper prayer and gives us the correct answers. So, we can get our answers by practicing communion, sharing with God through prayer and hearing back from Him through meditation and quietness (1 Kings 19:13). Make it a practice to pay attention to the Holy Spirit; witness in your spirit when you get the notification that your prayer has been heard. Then, if you can share your heart with God, make time for God to share His.

Option Two: The Way of the Creation

There are two sides to this coin we are about to discuss. The first is that an unbeliever can take any of the methods discussed here and gain results without "really consulting God." The second is that God may use the same way to lead His children; hence, the necessity of discussing this option.

We will use a car as the study's premise for the first side of the coin. This method studies the car, that is, letting the car talk back to us about why it is and its capabilities. This method doesn't consult the manufacturer and thus seems easier; however, there are things we may only know if the car goes through something that needs that feature. This method is simply reinventing the wheel, which is a waste of time. Yes, we may get answers, but at what cost? Such is the option that many people tend to choose. Some fear dealing with the manufacturer, so they opt for this. Others do not want to give the manufacturer "control," so they believe this option gives them control. However, this gained control is an illusion. I say that because no matter how we try, we can never know a car more than the manufacturer.

We might wonder why this was an option if it is so limiting. However, God's love for humanity makes certain essentials of life available to even those that do not know Him yet (Matthew 5:45). For example, all good and perfect gifts, including healings, come from God (James 1:17), yet He made medical science available. Therefore, the answer to that question is simply because of love (Romans 5:8). This way, those not saved can still know a bit of themselves and attain certain heights. What a loving God. This section will discuss how a simple man may find answers to the existential question without "really consulting" God.

The second side of the coin is where God leads us to one of these ways, or we employ this way with God involved. God may also use it to train us. Thus, this method should never be the primary way for the children of God. However, we can treat it as a supplemental method that God may use to lead.

Look at the Arsenal

For which of you, intending to build a tower, does not sit down first and count the cost, whether he has enough to finish it. Luke 14:28

In speaking to the disciples, Jesus alluded to the fact that we need to start any project by looking at our arsenal. It is an excellent step in any research. For our scenario here, we can translate the scripture above as such: *For which of you, intending to be great, does not sit down first and count his/her strengths and weaknesses, whether he/she has enough to be great.* Therefore, one significant way to get the answer to this question is to count our strengths and weaknesses. In other words, what do I have that sets me apart? What am I good at? These are the strengths. What do I have that makes me weak? A deep dive into our nature like this would help us know ourselves more and why we were created.

We should approach this as though we are conducting research. Follow the research procedures with you being the topic of the study. Search for information from reliable and authentic sources (including God through prayer and people). After which, we can analyze the information gathered and write a report. From this account, we can see a common denominator and a recommendation. Whatever our strength is geared towards is often an indication of our mini destiny. Locating these strengths and weaknesses is a form of *preparing our outside work, making it fit for ourselves in the field, and afterward, we can build our house* (Proverbs 24:27). This can be a starting point with the potential of unravelling our destiny.

Study the Patterns

"One witness shall not rise against a man concerning any iniquity or any sin that he commits; by the mouth of two or three witnesses the matter shall be established. Deuteronomy 19:15

This will be the third time I am coming to you. "By the mouth of two or three witnesses every word shall be established." 2 Corinthians 13:1

In the scriptures above, we see an essential and unchanging principle of the Kingdom of God. This way of doing things spans from the Old to the New Testament and is still in effect today. God sticks to it and expects us to do the same. It is the way things are done spiritually in dealing with God. In this way, we see that nothing is established in the supernatural (that is, the spiritual) without two or more witnesses. To expound this principle further, let us look at this practical example sighted by Jesus.

Moreover, if your brother sins against you, go and tell him about his fault between you and him alone. If he hears you, you have gained your brother. But if he will not hear, take with you one or two more, that 'by the mouth of two or three witnesses every word may be established.' And if he refuses to hear them, tell it to the church. But if he refuses even to hear the church, let him be to you like a heathen and a tax collector. Matthew 18:15-17.

Jesus gave us a clear example using this witness principle. If Jesus recommended this to us and the goal is for us to be like God (1 Peter 1:16), He must be gearing us toward something God does. Therefore, contrary to the notion that God rats people out, especially when we make a mistake, He does not. As explained by Jesus, when we sin against God, He comes to us one-on-one through the conviction of the Holy Spirit. If we refuse to listen, He convicts us again; but now, a witness may be involved, such as a prophet or a seemingly random word through teaching or preaching or otherwise. If we still refuse to listen, He reports us to our spiritual authority, such as Spiritual or biological parents or spiritual mentors. If we refuse to listen after this, it is established that we are sinners and no longer in God. So, Jesus asked us to follow the pattern God already employs. It is one way we utilize the principle to remain righteous and be like God.

We saw another variation of this principle again in Psalm 62:11, *God has spoken once, twice I have heard this: That power belongs to God.* There is usually an echo of the supernatural at least twice in the natural. Thus, anything that occurs in the natural at least twice could be an echo of the supernatural. We must pay attention.

In the same way, we can utilize this godly principle to answer existential questions. Whatever happens to us twice or more is an invitation to investigate. For example, suppose we keep doing something consistently and get the correct result. In that case, this can indicate that we should pursue that mini destiny. For example, an individual that walks past the homeless and is drawn emotionally every single time may be experiencing the effect of an echo of a homeless ministry calling. We can deduce our mini destinies by taking note of these patterns and investigating them (through prayer).

The indicators

As discussed, God, in His love, has put a system in place for all humans to deduce a portion of our purpose. These systems are the indicators placed in our being by God to point us in the right direction. Just as dashboard lights are an indicator of something (good or bad) in a car, so are these indicators in humans.

One of the ways we can confirm things of God is by what indicator(s) accompany the event or experience. These indicators are listed in Galatians 5:22-23.

But the fruit of the Spirit is love, joy, peace, longsuffering, gentleness, goodness, faith, meekness, temperance: against such there is no law.

When these indicators come on, we may be on a good trail. In the same way, some indicators can also tell us when the devil is behind a thing (See Galatians 5:19-21). Though there are many indicators, as seen above, we will only explore the three common indicators: Joy, Love and Peace.

Joy

Like the other indicators, Joy is a God phenomenon because it is found in the presence of God (Psalm 16:11). Unless God is in a place, that place is incapable of exhibiting joy. Therefore, to receive anything from God, joy is an absolute requirement (Isaiah 12:3). The devil does not have joy, nor can he produce it. He can't even fake these and the other indicators properly. Only God has the hallmark, monopoly, and exclusivity to joy. Therefore, whatever brings joy, is God, and whatever brings sorrow is the devil. As the scripture shows, joy is evidence of God's presence and sanction. Thus, it is essential to understand the concept of joy.

What is joy? Contrary to the common mistake that some of us make, joy and happiness are not the same. The name happiness implies that it is based on happenings. Therefore, something must happen to cause happiness. But, on the other hand, joy is not generated by us or anything that happens. It is given to us by God, circumstance and situation notwithstanding. Yes, we can express joy through our feelings, but it is the perpetual state of the heart. We know we are in joy when we are content and joyful despite the result or bad happenings. So, whatever we do that brings this feeling consistently, even sometimes despite the losses, may indicate a purpose that will bring us before kings if we are diligent (Proverbs 22:29). Joy is a connector to the Maker's will for us.

Love

Another important indicator is love. We know this points us in the right direction because God is love (1 John 4:8).

So, anything of God is of love, and we are of God (1 John 4:4). Thus, when we follow the procedure of this indicator as listed in Mark 12:30-31, that is, God first and ourselves and others, we will get the results. As such, whatever we find ourselves loving can indicate what God has in mind for us. Though there are many definitions of love today, the love we are talking about is an emotional phenomenon that lets us do things without fear (1 John 4:18) nor for selfish ambition (1 Corinthians 13:5). Therefore, anything that we do out of fear or for selfish reasons, is not of love. Yes, doing what we love might benefit us, but that was not the motive. So, whatever we engage in, that makes us fearless and selfless is worth emphasizing. The key to this is to analyze our hearts sincerely. We should ask ourselves, why do we love doing what we do? Do we enjoy it? And does it bring the feeling of fulfilment? When what we feel is satisfaction and accompanied by any other indicator, we are up to something.

Peace

From Isaiah 9:6, we know that one of the names of Jesus is the Prince of Peace. Therefore, if Jesus is the prince, God is the King of Peace. When God shows up, He is accompanied by peace for those on His good side. This peace is not always the absence of trouble but rather the calmness of heart, even in trouble (See John 16:33). Therefore, *when a man's ways please the Lord, He makes even his enemies to be at peace with him.* Proverbs 16:7. This is so because peace flows from God to all things. When we are at peace, then we are on track. Where peace ends is where God stops. We must pay attention to this godly indicator to please God and walk in His ways. Whatever we consistently find peace and solace in can indicate that God is involved.

In summary, we may deduce things from these individual indicators, but I strongly recommend having two or three witnesses of these indicators. For example, what we love may also bring us joy before making a solid decision. It is because, ideally, whatever is from God will be accompanied by all these indicators simultaneously; we may just be tuned to pick one signal over the others first. But whatever we pick, we only decide once we pick another indicator signal.

The Passion Figure

Google defines passion as a *strong and barely controllable emotion*. The qualification of being barely controllable is valid because what we are passionate about, we often don't think before we act. Passion is often a zeal that pushes us to action rather than to think. Though this is a bad thing in some cases, in others, it is precisely what we need to get things done. Almost every skill can be learnt and taught. But Passion cannot be taught or learnt. When we lack passion for something, we cannot do it excellently.

Therefore, whatever we find ourselves passionate about means we've not been taught nor learnt the passion, but it has come from our depth. In Matthew 6:21, Jesus said for where our treasure is, there our heart will also be. Passion is a product of our heart. So, wherever it points us is worth investigating. Zeal and passion for something indicate that there might be a hidden treasure in that thing.

In conclusion, as alluded to earlier, any method in option two can answer the existential question. However, to be sure of our answer, we must consult God and let Him lead us. Venturing into any of the methods listed here can be a hit or miss. Such is because, without God, we depend on humans to interpret things accurately, which as humans, is not guaranteed. Hence the tolerances and human error factors in research processes. Simply put, accuracy is impossible without God.

The Purpose

Therefore, whether you eat or drink, or whatever you do, do all to the glory of God. 1 Corinthians 10:31

We must discuss an important concept before we close out the chapter. It is the purpose of finding ourselves. Yes, this will help us focus and achieve heights on earth, which is the dominion, but it goes beyond that. In addition to what was discussed extensively in chapter one, the purpose of all destinies is for God's glory (1 Corinthians 10:31). As we have established, God made us the way we are with talents and abilities (See Matthew 25:14-30). But, like an employer who sends an employee on a developmental course, there is an expectation. Yes, God expects us to dominate the earth (Genesis 1:28); but He wants us to do so for His glory.

It is imperative because we are created for God's glory (Isaiah 43:7). Therefore, whatever we do should be for His glory. It is so because *in Him we live and move and have our being, as also some of your own poets have said, 'For we are also His offspring.'* (Acts 17:28). So, whatever we do on earth, we can do because of God. Giving glory to God doesn't mean He lacks it or we are adding to His glory; no, it is for our benefit. Most dictionaries agree that glory means honor. God made us with talents and abilities that put us in dominion on earth. Therefore, the least we can do is honor Him in all we do. Just like we shout out to our sponsors, giving God glory can be viewed as such. We can practically do this by recognizing Him, acknowledging Him (Proverbs 3:6), and whatever we do is pleasing to Him (Colossians 3:17). True honor comes from a place of reverence. Therefore, it is impossible to give glory to God (honor) without the fear of God (reverence).

Yes, those that do not fear God may "find themselves" and attain some heights on earth. However, this is dangerous because, *surely, they are set in slippery places; they will be cast down to destruction. Oh, how they will be brought to desolation, as in a moment! They will be utterly consumed with terrors.* Psalm 73:18-19, rephrased. Also, *the wealth of the sinner is stored up for the righteous* (Proverbs 13:22b). These scriptures show us that there is no way to remain consistently at that height without acknowledging God. Those who do not fear God enough to acknowledge Him are deemed wicked (Ecclesiastes 8:13); their end will be worse than their beginning. There are many examples today of many wealthy people who die of sickness. I am not saying that God did this, but I am saying that by not acknowledging God, He has no obligation to protect us from evil.

In conclusion, to acknowledge God starts with Romans 10:9-10. *If you confess with your mouth the Lord Jesus and believe in your heart that God has raised Him from the dead, you will be saved. For with the heart one believes unto righteousness, and with the mouth, confession is made unto salvation.* We can do this by saying the new believer's prayer at the end of the book. May God bless and help you in Jesus' name. Amen

Chapter 3

Stay in Your Lane

Blow the trumpet in Zion and sound an alarm in My holy mountain! Let all the inhabitants of the land tremble; For the day of the Lord is coming, for it is at hand: A Day of darkness and gloominess, A Day of clouds and thick darkness, Like the morning clouds spread over the mountains. A people come, great and strong, the like of whom has never been nor will there ever be any such after them, even for many successive generations. A fire devours before them, and behind them a flame burns; The land is like the Garden of Eden before them, and behind them a desolate wilderness; Surely nothing shall escape them. Their appearance is like the appearance of horses; And like swift steeds, so they run. With a noise like chariots Over mountaintops they leap, Like the noise of a flaming fire that devours the stubble, like a strong people set in battle array. Before them the people writhe in pain; All faces are drained of color. They run like mighty men, they climb the wall like men of war; Everyone marches in formation, and they do not break ranks. They do not push one another; Everyone marches in his own column. Though they lunge between the weapons, they are not cut down. They run to and fro in the city, they run on the wall; They climb into the houses, they enter at the windows like a thief. The earthquakes before them, the heavens tremble; The sun and moon grow dark, And the stars diminish their brightness. The Lord gives voice before His army, For His camp is very great; For strong is the One who executes His word. For the day of the Lord is great and very terrible; Who can endure it? Joel 2:1-11

In this chapter, we will discuss the essential ingredients to greatness. We will deduce it from the scripture above. From Hosea 4:6, we know that knowledge is crucial to greatness. What we have learnt thus far are critical parts of our journey to greatness; however, we must take the steps and implement what we have learnt to be great and have dominion. What we know and the information we have are there so we can make informed decisions.

From the scripture above, there are a few things to note. The first is that God planned to bring about "The day of the Lord ."Due to this, He chose and sent a people, great and strong, the like of whom has never been nor will there ever be any such after them, even for many successive generations. We have discussed this in Chapters 1 and 2. The next stage, from Joel 2, is God gave the how. He gave the people how to achieve what He was sending them to do. For this stage, we can implement the same principle introduced in Chapter 2: to study the call and how to achieve the goal. The third stage, which is the focus of this chapter, is that *everyone marches in formation* and *they do not break ranks. They do not push one another; everyone marches in his column.* Now let us analyze each of these and deduce what they mean for us today.

March in Formation

To march in formation is an interesting metaphor because the most disciplined entity on earth today is the military. As per Paul the Apostle, in 2 Timothy 2:3-4, we are soldiers. God expects a military-style discipline and even more from His children, especially those He has called and chosen (Matthew 22:14). Any soldier that will fulfil a purpose and carry out command successfully, especially in battle, must be a part of a group of soldiers or troops, in formation. Such is known as a phalanx. Therefore, in preparation for battle, the first thing a soldier is assigned is their formation. All they do is within their assigned group. Thus, it is not a coincidence that if we are to fulfil destiny, we must be part of a formation.

The Bible made us understand in Ephesians 6:12 that *we do not wrestle against flesh and blood, but against principalities, against powers, against the rulers of the darkness of this age, against spiritual hosts of wickedness in the heavenly places.* And 1 Peter 5:8, we are advised to *be sober, be vigilant; because your adversary the devil walks about like a roaring lion, seeking whom he may devour.* These two scriptures made us understand that there is a battle to fight on our way to greatness. As such, we need to march in formation to win the battle. Such understanding, therefore, begs the question, what is our formation as children of God, and how do we march in it?

WHAT IS A FORMATION?

We will start our discussion by defining formation and deducing what it is for us from the scriptures. As per Merriam-Webster dictionary, a formation is *the arrangement of a body or group of persons or things in some prescribed manner or for a particular purpose.* Few things to note here, it is a group of persons or, in our case, soldiers. So, they all have something in common. Secondly, it is for a particular purpose. It implies that many formations within one military may exist for many different purposes. Also, each soldier's capability is geared towards the goal of the formation. Lastly, if this is a requirement, the term "lone ranger" is a fallacy and a product of pride. There is no such thing as a soldier acting without being part of a group, not in the earthly military nor is it right in God's kingdom. We must all be part of a group, a formation.

Thus, Hebrews 10:25 says *not forsaking the assembling of ourselves together, as is the manner of some, but exhorting one another, and so much the more as you see the Day approaching.* Putting this scripture in context, it will read like this: *as soldiers, we are not to forsake our formation, as is the manner of some, but march together to perfect the craft and so much more as we prepare for the Day of battle.* Therefore, the church of Christ is the only thing that fits the description of a formation that is a group of like-minded people with a collective goal. Now to put this in perspective, the military, in this case, will be the body of Christ. At the same time, the formation will be the individual churches within the body. Therefore, the church is the formation that every soldier of Christ today must be a part of.

In this way, we understand why it is necessary to have various churches within the body of Christ. Each God-ordained formation, that is, a church, is assigned a purpose and a goal. Everyone assigned to that formation is thereby tasked to use what they possess to achieve that goal.

So, after we have located our mini destinies, the next thing is that we find our formation. There is not a single soldier that operates outside of a formation in battle. To do so is to invite danger to themselves and other military members. Therefore, the soldiers in a formation see themselves as family. In the same way, anybody with any call, either king or priest, must belong to a formation, a household of God (Ephesians 2:19).

Per the military rules, no soldier can choose their formation, but the superior decides what formation they'll be in. In the same way, every formation in the body of Christ has an assigned head called a Shepherd. Per Jeremiah 3:15, the Lord, the head of the church (Colossians 1:18), purchases it with His blood (Acts 20:28) and gives each person a shepherd. This process indicates what formation/church we ought to belong. We can employ the steps presented in Chapter 2 to approach God for this as well; however, only God has the right to put us in a formation.

HOW DO WE MARCH IN A FORMATION?

For as the body is one and has many members, but all the members of that one body, being many, are one body, so also is Christ. For by one Spirit, we were all baptized into one body—whether Jews or Greeks, whether slaves or free—and have all been made to drink into one Spirit. For in fact the body is not one member but many. If the foot should say, "Because I am not a hand, I am not of the body," is it therefore not of the body? And if the ear should say, "Because I am not an eye, I am not of the body," is it therefore not of the body? If the whole body were an eye, where would be the hearing? If the whole were hearing, where would be the smelling? But now God has set the members, each one of them, in the body just as He pleased. And if they were all one member, where would the body be? But now indeed there are many members, yet one body. And the eye cannot say to the hand, "I have no need of you"; nor again the head to the feet, "I have no need of you." No, much rather, those members of the body which seem to be weaker are necessary. And those members of the body which we think to be less honorable, on these we bestow greater honor; and our unpresentable parts have greater modesty, but our presentable parts have no need. But God composed the body, having given greater honor to that part which lacks it, that there should be no schism in the body, but that the members should have the same care for one another. And if one member suffers, all the members suffer with it; or if one member is honored, all the members rejoice with it. Now you are the body of Christ, and members individually. And God has appointed these in the church: first apostles, second prophets, third teachers, after that miracle, then gifts of healings, helps, administrations, varieties of tongues. Are all apostles? Are all prophets? Are all teachers? Are all workers of miracles? Do all have gifts of healings? Do all speak with tongues? Do all interpret? 1 Corinthians 12:12-30.

The scripture above is the summary of how we march within the formation. Every member of a formation is critical. There is no one member without a purpose; therefore, the members are all needed no matter how big a formation is. There is no passive member in a formation; they are all active members. Marching in a formation is an action word. In the same vein, to be part of a church is to be an active and not passive member. We must start by understanding the goal of the formation and how they fit into the overall military. Since a formation that does not align with the overall goal of the military is a rebellious one. As such, we must avoid it like the plague. Once we know this, we must find out how we fit into the formation. We can do so by speaking to God directly or to the Shepherd. We must then be willing to utilize what we possess to bring about the goal of the formation. We must be known, and we must contribute. To march in formation is to serve within the church in any capacity that aligns with the mini destinies we have uncovered (1 Peter 4:10-11, Ephesians 4:11-16 & Romans 12:6-8).

We must note that though every member is necessary, any person can be replaced if they are not marching. There is no indispensable member in a formation. My father in the Lord coined a phrase by the Spirit of God: "*God's purpose does not change, but the people can.*" For every Saul, there is always a David on the sideline. Such is because the goal of the formation must be achieved. So, being part is not enough; marching in formation is what matters.

To march within a formation is to be part of a local church that knows and identifies with you. Whatever your calling is (king and/or priest), you must benefit the body of Christ and be a part of the church.

WHY DO WE NEED TO MARCH IN FORMATION?

There are many reasons we must march in formation, but we will only discuss a few for our studies here.

To End Up with Christ Eternally

Husbands, love your wives, just as Christ also loved the church and gave Himself for her, that He might sanctify and cleanse her with the washing of water by the word, that He might present her to Himself a glorious church, not having spot or wrinkle or any such thing, but that she should be holy and without blemish. Ephesians 5:25-27

From the scripture above, only those who are part of a church will be presented as a glorious church. Hence, any soldier not part of a formation cannot be part of the victory parade and/or endowments. To be presented as a glorious, clean church, some procedures must be done within that formation. This way, *nothing unclean will ever enter it, nor anyone who does what is detestable or false, but only those who are written in the Lamb's book of life.* Revelation 21:27 ESV. Therefore, anybody not part of the formation cannot be a part of the process needed for cleansing, standing at the risk of losing the fight altogether and ending up in hell. If we do not belong to the body of Christ—the Church (Ephesians 5:29), we can have no part, neither in Christ nor the place, He went to prepare (John 14:2).

To Give glory to God

In the previous chapter, we explained that our destiny's purpose is to bring glory to God. We went further to say that we give glory to God when we honor and revere Him. To honor God is to acknowledge Him, and to do it with the right motive is reverence. We can do this in a few ways:

Obedience

Obedience is to support God's ways and acts and obey His commands. Since all scriptures are God's breath (2 Timothy 3:16), by obeying Hebrews 10:25, which says *not to forsake the assembling of ourselves together*, we are bringing God glory. Thus, John 14:23 says, *If anyone loves Me, he will keep My word; and My Father will love him, and We will come to him and make Our home with him.* Obedience is one of the ways we honor God and revere Him.

Believe

In Romans 10:9, we saw that the premise of our salvation is on confessing and believing. Such means to acknowledge with reverence what God has done for us through Jesus. In the same vein, by being part of and marching in a formation—a church that cost Christ His blood (Acts 20:28), we believe (acknowledging) God's work for and in that formation and thereby honoring Him. Such again brings glory to God.

Identification

In Matthew 10:33 and Luke 12:9, Jesus made us understand that whoever does not identify with Him, He will not identify with such a person in front of His Father and His angels. The church of God is the body of Christ (Ephesians 5:29). It is one of the significant ways we identify with Christ. We identify with that formation and its head when we belong to a formation. Jesus is the head of the church (Colossians 1:18 & Ephesians 1:22). This means that when we identify with a formation, the church, we identify with Jesus and with God who sent Him (John 12:49). In this way, identification is a way we honor God, thereby bringing Him glory.

To Win Battles

The world we live in is that of battles. Jesus affirmed this in John 16:33 when He said *in the world you will have tribulation, but be of good cheer, I have overcome the world.* From this, we understand that we will have battles to fight, but unlike some beliefs, *we do not wrestle (fight) against flesh and blood, but against principalities, against powers, against the rulers of the darkness of this age, against spiritual hosts of wickedness in the heavenly places* (Ephesians 6:12, emphasis mine).

From John 16:33 and Romans 8:37, we saw that battles are a must for us and the only sure way to fight and win is through Jesus. It is a sure win because Jesus won already (Colossians 2:15, 1 Corinthians 15:57 & Romans 8:37); we appropriate it. Therefore, through salvation and becoming part of the body of Christ, we have a guarantee of winning every battle. Being part of a formation does not stop battles but guarantees winnings (See Mark 4:35-41).

Furthermore, most predators that are successful in their quest do so in packs. From grey wolves to lions, even hyenas, they all hunt in packs. Such is because there is strength in numbers. The more the number, the more the power. We have a better chance for strategy and contribution. Jesus said in Matthew 18:19, *if (at least) two of you agree on earth concerning anything that they ask, it will be done for them by My Father in heaven*. Such means it will be done when at least two people come together in a formation and put in their strength towards something. Such is because *where two or three are gathered together in My name, I am there in the midst of them* (Matthew 18:20). Every formation in the body of Christ carries the presence of Jesus. As such, winning is a guarantee (Psalm 24:7-10 & 114:3-7).

In this way, if a formation (the church) faces a battle as one, they are bound to win. In addition, we learnt in 1 Corinthians 12:26 *that if one member suffers, all the members suffer with it; or if one member is honored, all the members rejoice with it*. Thus, we are bound to win when we are part of a formation. So, for as long as we are part of the formation, winning is guaranteed. Do you want to win every battle that comes your way? Then be saved, as per Romans 10:9, and be part of a church.

Finally, *two are better than one because they have a good reward for their labor. For if they fall, one will lift up his companion. But woe to him who is alone when he falls, for he has no one to help him up* (Ecclesiastes 4:10). In a formation like the body of Christ, which is built on love, we are lifted, strengthened, and encouraged. We can tap into strength to win battles.

Do not Break Ranks

If the foot should say, "Because I am not a hand, I am not of the body," is it therefore not of the body? And if the ear should say, "Because I am not an eye, I am not of the body," is it therefore not of the body? If the whole body were an eye, where would be the hearing? If the whole were hearing, where would be the smelling? But now God has set the members, each one of them, in the body just as He pleased. And if they were all one member, where would the body be? But now indeed there are many members, yet one body. And the eye cannot say to the hand, "I have no need of you"; nor again the head to the feet, "I have no need of you." No, much rather, those members of the body which seem to be weaker are necessary. And those members of the body which we think to be less honorable, on these we bestow greater honor; and our unpresentable parts have greater modesty, but our presentable parts have no need. But God composed the body, having given greater honor to that part which lacks it, that there should be no schism in the body, but that the members should have the same care for one another. And if one member suffers, all the members suffer with it; or if one member is honored, all the members rejoice with it. 1 Corinthians 12:15-26

We have established that one main reason for the formation (the church) is so *that He (Jesus) might present her (the church) to Himself a glorious church, not having spot or wrinkle or any such thing, but that she should be holy and without blemish* (Ephesians 5:27, emphasis mine). For this to happen, every member of the body must know and assume their place within the body. Therefore, God has given us *shepherds according to His heart, who will feed us with knowledge and understanding* (Jeremiah 3:15). This establishes that at the top of this hierarchy is the human shepherd, the Church Pastor. He has also given the church *some to be apostles, some prophets, some evangelists, and some pastors and teachers for the equipping of the saints for the work of ministry, for the edifying of the body of Christ, till we all come to the unity of the faith and of the knowledge of the Son of God, to a perfect man, to the measure of the stature of the fullness of Christ* (Ephesians 4:11-12). From these scriptures, we can deduce five hierarchies within the formation. Within these hierarchies, every member of the formation has been assigned to by God. We went into deeper details in Chapter 1.

Thus, the moment we join a formation, we must figure out our rank based on what we have deduced about ourselves. Also, we must figure out the hierarchy and the right ways of doing things. Such is because it is our responsibility, and there is no ignorance of the law. Ranks, as per Google, in terms of the military, is *a position in the armed forces hierarchy.* In the same way, our rank is the position God has chosen us to occupy in the hierarchy of the formation. Due to these facts, two significant ways we can break ranks exist. The first is to leave a formation or not be a part of a formation. As we have established, under no circumstance is a child of God allowed to be alive without being part of a church. Therefore, the day we do this, we break ranks. The second way is to dishonor or disregard the chain of command within the formation. We have explained the first in *March in Formation*; however, we will drill down into the second.

THE CHAIN OF COMMAND

Then Miriam and Aaron spoke against Moses because of the Ethiopian woman whom he had married; for he had married an Ethiopian woman. So, they said, "Has the Lord indeed spoken only through Moses? Has He not spoken through us also?" And the Lord heard it. (Now the man Moses was very humble, more than all men who were on the face of the earth. Suddenly the Lord said to Moses, Aaron, and Miriam, "Come out, you three, to the tabernacle of meeting!" So, the three came out. Then the Lord came down in the pillar of cloud and stood in the door of the tabernacle and called Aaron and Miriam. And they both went forward. Then He said, "Hear now My words: If there is a prophet among you, I, the Lord, make Myself known to him in a vision; I speak to him in a dream. Not so with My servant Moses, He is faithful in all My house. I speak with him face to face, even plainly, and not in dark sayings; And he sees the form of the Lord. Why then were you not afraid. To speak against My servant Moses?" So, the anger of the Lord was aroused against them, and He departed. And when the cloud departed from above the tabernacle, suddenly Miriam became leprous, as white as snow. Then Aaron turned toward Miriam, and there she was, a leper. So, Aaron said to Moses, "Oh, my lord! Please do not lay this sin on us, in which we have done foolishly and in which we have sinned. Please do not let her be as one dead, whose flesh is half consumed when he comes out of his mother's womb!" So, Moses cried out to the Lord, saying, "Please heal her, O God, I pray!" Then the Lord said to Moses, "If her father had but spit in her face, would she not be shamed seven days? Let her be shut out of the camp seven days, and afterward she may be received again." So, Miriam was shut out of the camp seven days, and the people did not journey till Miriam was brought in again. And afterward the people moved from Hazeroth and camped in the Wilderness of Paran. Numbers 12:1-16

The scripture above is an eye-opener. According to the word of the Lord, as seen in Deuteronomy 7:3 and many others, God does not condone intermarriages with non-Israelites, that is, non-believers. Miriam and Aaron were right; however, they did it in a rebellious form. They disregarded Moses, who happened to outrank them and had more authority. They broke rank by nursing a coup. The statement *Has the Lord indeed spoken only through Moses? Has He not spoken through us also?* Revealed the posture of comparison and rebellion in their heart. The devil uttered a variation of this statement in Isaiah 14:13, leading to his eviction from heaven.

God is a God of orderliness (1 Corinthians 14:33). Due to this fact, he has placed authorities everywhere we find ourselves. Without authority and hierarchy, we cannot achieve order. Thus, if there is one thing He cannot stand, it is rebellion. To break rank is to rebel. Another scripture that gives us insight into this is Numbers 16, where three people revolted against Moses. In this case, they and their families suffered the consequences.

In conclusion, the only reason a being was kicked out of heaven was for rebellion. The true meaning of breaking ranks is insubordination and mutiny. As we have alluded to, God places us in a formation and determines the hierarchy. So, if we have issues with how things are done, take it up with Him or present your case to the appropriate authority with honor. Do not engage in gossip, planning a coup, etc. These are tools of hell, and as such, God will fight for His church and those He has placed in authority (Matthew 16:18). God showed up for Moses because he didn't put himself in the formation nor the rank; God did. In the same way, when we engage in these rank-breaking actions, we are fighting God, who has set up the formation and ranks. May God help us in Jesus' name. Amen

Do not Push Others

A few years ago, the Lord asked me a simple question. He said, do you know how many planes are flying right now? I answered no. He responded, go, and check. So I pulled out my laptop and checked. To my surprise, thousands of planes were flying over North America alone. Some of them even seemed as though they were on a course to collide, but that was not the case. It was before the Covid-19 pandemic. As I write this book, I decided to check again; there are still over 5000 planes flying over North America, despite the ravaging pandemic. As I looked on, the Lord continued to speak to me. He said, son if humans can build a system that allows so many planes to fly simultaneously, over the same area, at the same altitude with little to no collision, do you think you have to push another to get to the top?

Contrary to what the world teaches, there are many ways to the top in God. As we have explored in Chapter 1, all mini-destinies have the potential to reach the top. Therefore, there is no need to envy others or push others down.

Before we go deeper, it is outside our purview if someone is to be replaced or put down. Whoever, you do not lift, you have no right to pull down. So the Bible said in Psalm 75:7 *but God is the Judge: He puts down one and exalts another.* This scripture is no excuse to put each other down. Instead, it shows us that it is simply in the purview of God. David did not pull Saul down, though he had much ammunition to use (1 Samuel 16:14-23). God rejected Saul and anointed David (1 Samuel 16:1). If Saul did not mess up, God would still have another place of dominion for David.

Here is a fact: anything from God has the potential to be at the top and enormous. The Bible made us understand, in Isaiah 66:1, that heaven is God's throne, and the earth is His footstool. If the whole earth is only a footstool, then we cannot begin to imagine how big God is or anything that comes from God. However, from the scriptures, after creation in Genesis, we can see that the principle of God dictates that whatever comes from Him starts small and grows gradually into its full potential. Jesus was born as a baby and grew into His potential (Matthew, Mark, Luke, and John). Thus, we were advised not to despise the days of humble beginnings (Zachariah 4:10). In this way, we see that anything big, without any traceable history of humble beginnings, is demonic. There is no godly glory without a story of little beginnings. So, whatever your lane is, your rank is, whatever it is you are destined for within the formation, if you hold on to it and perfect your craft, your place is at the top. Every option in God leads to greatness.

COMPLEMENT NOT COMPETE

Yet if your brother is grieved because of your food, you are no longer walking in love. Do not destroy with your food the one for whom Christ died. Therefore, do not let your good be spoken of as evil; for the kingdom of God is not eating and drinking, but righteousness and peace and joy in the Holy Spirit. For he who serves Christ in these things is acceptable to God and approved by men. Therefore, let us pursue the things which make for peace and the things by which one may edify another. Do not destroy the work of God for the sake of food. All things indeed are pure, but it is evil for the man who eats with offense. It is good neither to eat meat nor drink wine nor do anything by which your brother stumbles or is offended or is made weak. Do you have faith? Have it to yourself before God. Happy is he who does not condemn himself in what he approves. But he who doubts is condemned if he eats, because he does not eat from faith; for whatever is not from faith is sin. Romans 14:15-23.

There are a few things to note from the scriptures above. The first corresponds with the fact that our faith is based on love. So, whatever we do that is born of hatred towards another violates this. Secondly, as a formation member, it is one of our responsibilities to see that we achieve the formation's goal. As we have noted, the goal is to be presented as a glorified and sanctified church. We accomplish this when we edify each other. Lastly, whatever we want to do that puts another person in danger of falling, we must avoid it. Such is because every person in the formation is the work of God; each of them costs God the blood of Jesus. So, let's drill into each one.

From the words of Jesus in Mark 12:30-31 and Apostle Paul's insight in Romans 13:10, the premise of our faith is love. From God sending Jesus (John 3:16) to humans remaining in God (Mark 12:30-31), we see the necessity of love. In this way, if we love one another in our formation as we love ourselves, we will not push them. We will understand that the fall of one within the formation is the fall of all (1 Corinthians 12:26 & Matthew 12:25). So, if we want success, then we must complement each other and not compete. We will have to push each other when we compete, and the last man standing wins. In the case of a formation, no one man is winning; it is us versus them. That is the body of Christ versus the kingdom of the devil. By pushing one another within the body, we create a loophole for the devil to take our formation down (Mark 3:24).

Secondly, there is no puzzle with the same puzzle pieces. Suppose we believe God doesn't make mistakes. In that case, every individual in a formation is a different piece needed for the puzzle. Competing with another piece is a simple definition of absurdity. It is because we aim to be the same puzzle piece, which is useless since we only need one. Doing so leaves the formation with a critical/needed piece short. For as long as your fingerprint is unique, the formation cannot be a complete puzzle without you in your place and what you have to offer. Therefore, each puzzle piece does its part to make it easier to locate where the other puzzle piece fits.

Consequently, we must make it easy for the next person in the formation. We do this by simply edifying one another. *If the foot should say, "Because I am not a hand, I am not of the body," is it therefore not of the body? And if the ear should say, "Because I am not an eye, I am not of the body," is it therefore not of the body? If the whole body were an eye, where would be the hearing? If the whole were hearing, where would be the smelling? But now God has set the members, each one of them, in the body just as He pleased. And if they were all one member, where would the body be?* 1 Corinthians 12:14-19.

Lastly, Jesus said in Luke 17:1 and Matthew 18:7 that woe to the one who happens to be a stumbling block for another. He went on to say, in Luke 17:2, that it is better for such individuals to stop existing than to be the reason another person fails. To put this in perspective, from 1 Peter 5:8, we know that the devil actively seeks to bring us down. When we push one another, we assume the devil's image by doing his job. As such, God will come at us as though we are the devil. It is because, in that moment, we are the extension of the devil.

March in Your Column

For as we have many members in one body, but all the members do not have the same function, so we, being many, are one body in Christ, and individually members of one another. Having then gifts differing according to the grace that is given to us, let us use them: if prophecy, let us prophecy in proportion to our faith; or ministry, let us use it in our ministering; he who teaches, in teaching; he who exhorts, in exhortation; he who gives, with liberality; he who leads, with diligence; he who shows mercy, with cheerfulness. Romans 12:4-8.

The totality of this portion of our studies is summarized in the scripture above. Like the subsection before, there is a need for formation members. As such, there is a column, portion, or path carved out for each member. From the scripture above, we see that every member of the body, and specifically formation, will have a different gift(s). Though some giftings might be similar, the mini goal always differs.

As established in Chapter 1, the destination for us all is the top, which is dominion. We achieve this either through kingship and/or priesthood. However, the path to this is through the fivefold offices, where everyone can locate themselves in one or multiple. But even within the fivefold, there are many paths. For example, we find shepherds, counsellors, nurses, and doctors under the pastoral umbrella, etc. Under each of these paths are also specialties; however, when we follow the steps outlined in chapter 2, we can zoom into our path and specialty to dominion.

Once we locate this path and specialties and are a part of a formation, we must know our column.

We deduce how to locate our column from the statement in these scriptures: *But to each one of us grace was given according to the measure of Christ's gift* (Ephesians 4:7). *Having then gifts differ according to the grace that is given to us* (Romans 12:6). We see that the gifts that we possess are accompanied by grace. Grace, which means supernatural help, is the extent of our column. It is grace that helps us function in our gifts. The grace made available to us is the freedom that we have. It is the lane God has designed for us; grace is the running track in this race to the top. It is the amount of allowance we have. In this way, your gift will determine your grace; therefore, anything we have no grace for, we have no gift for and vice versa. Grace is the column that God has given us to march in.

Though we have the track allowance, most runners utilize only some of it. It is the same for the spiritual sprint as well. Though it is possible to use our gifts to the total allowance of grace, this is practically done through faith. Therefore, *if prophecy, let us prophecy in proportion to our faith* (Romans 12:6). Grace says from here to there, you can run, while faith is the actual thing we do. For example, grace says you have an allowance of 30, but the amount of the 30 we use is based on our faith. So, we utilize our gift through faith, but this we do within the allowance of grace.

From our discussion thus far, we see that there is grace according to the measure of gift and the right way to utilize gift is through faith. It reveals that there is a faith component to all of this. As per Hebrews 11:1: *faith is the substance of things hoped for, the evidence of things not seen.* In other words, it is the assurance that we have what we are hoping for. To have such assurance, one must have seen it happen; but as per the definition, this is impossible. As such, faith is supplied by God, who already knows the end from the beginning (Isaiah 46:10). He does this through His word (Romans 10:17). So, to operate to the fulness of our column, we must spend time in God's word to understand the extent of our grace. This exercise builds the correct quantity of faith needed for our giftings. Thus, Romans 12:3 made us know that *though grace is given, God has dealt to each one a measure of faith.*

In summary, every mini destiny from God comes with grace. Where our faith starts and stops at each point can indicate the column we are marching in. Our faith is our restriction, and we operate (march) within our level of faith; however, the grace that accompanies the gift is God's column for us. Hence, the most preferred way is for us to keep growing in our faith until we reach the fullness of the grace given (See Proverbs 4:18 & John 14:12).

Diligence

Seest thou a man diligent in his business? he shall stand before kings; he shall not stand before mean men. Proverbs 22:29 KJV

From the scripture above, the force that brings us before kings, that is, dominion is diligence; therefore, it becomes a critical part of our studies.

Diligence is the binding ingredient for everything we have discussed thus far. If diligence is present, we can achieve the dominion results. By trading with this critical building block, we are destined to be in the company of rulers, which is dominion.

Google defines diligence as careful and persistent work or effort. I describe it as the ability to work to achieve a goal persistently. From these definitions, work and persistence stood out. Let us take each one and analyze them.

WORK OR EFFORT

From our studies, we have deduced that though grace is given, faith determines the extent of grace we utilize. Therefore, if we are to have dominion, faith is a necessity. In this way, our current level of dominion is the current level of our faith. As per James 2:17, "faith without works is dead." It implies that what makes faith alive to yield results is work. In this way, we see that work gives life to faith. In the same way, knowing our mini destinies without putting in the necessary work will keep us in slavery. So to attain dominion, we must achieve the fullness of grace that God has given to us. We must utilize the totality of the grace made available to us by God. To do this, we must increase our faith, and to increase our faith; we must increase our work. We must effectively balance faith and work to achieve God's vision for our life. Therefore, the saying is true, "the result of good work is more work." As such, *everyone to whom much is given, from him much will be required; and to whom much has been committed, of him they will ask the more.* Luke 12:48.

Since *faith comes by hearing and hearing by the word of God* (Romans 10:17), and *faith without works is dead* (James 2:17), this implies that the prescribed works needed for faith are in God's word. So, we must hear from God to locate the right works to activate and increase faith.

PERSISTENCE

From Google, we see the definition of persistence as *the firm or obstinate continuance in the course of action despite difficulty or opposition.* It is doing what we ought to do repeatedly, in the face of opposition, until we get the correct result. It is not the same as insanity, defined as doing the same thing and expecting a different result. Persistence denotes wisdom, while insanity denotes foolishness. For persistence, we have evidence that the work can produce results, so we keep at it until it fulfils its potential. So, persistence becomes essential and critical once we locate the proper work. True diligence comes because of persistence. It is excellence that makes us rule in our lane, and persistence is needed for excellence.

In explaining this concept as it relates to prayer (a form of right works), Jesus sighted a parable worth analyzing in Luke 18:1-5.

Then He spoke a parable to them, that men always ought to pray (do right works) and not lose heart, saying: "There was in a certain city a judge who did not fear God nor regard man. Now there was a widow in that city; and she came to him, saying, 'Get justice for me from my adversary.' And he would not for a while; but afterward he said within himself, 'Though I do not fear God nor regard man, yet because this widow troubles me I will avenge her, lest by her continual coming she weary me.'"

For the sake of our study, we will analyze a benefit of persistence here. Many know that persistence in the right work will make us the best in our field. As such, we will rule; however, the inner working of this was what Jesus revealed to us in the parable above. As per 2 Corinthians 4:4, the devil is the god of this world. Such was why he could say to Jesus in Matthew 4:8-9 that he would give Him the kingdom of this world. Jesus never objected because that was a fact. So, persistence is a practical key if we are to be the head in a world ruled by the devil. For our study, the devil is the judge who does not fear God nor regard man in the parable. A widow, in this case, is someone without any help. As believers, we are not helpless because we have God on our side; however, if a widow can get results using this tactic, we cannot begin to comprehend the benefit we stand to gain. Even those without God can get results in this world. As we persist in the right works, we are troubling the god of this world and weary him. He will have no choice but to make room for us to attain the height God destined for us.

Chapter 4

The Strategy of the Devil

We have discussed the options and how to find where we belong; however, all that is simply information. Though this is important (Hosea 4:6), the Bible, in 1 Peter 5:8, also commands us to *be sober, be vigilant because your adversary, the devil, walks about like a roaring lion, seeking whom he may devour.* It implies that we cannot let our guard down at any time; the devil is always after us intending to steal, kill and destroy (John 10:10). The more we know, the more the target is on our back (1 Corinthians 10:13). This means every time we are given information, we should expect temptations on what we've just been given. *For everyone to whom much is given, from him much will be required; and to whom much has been committed, of him they will ask the more* (Luke 12:48b). Often, the devil may fail at stopping a person from getting the right information; in these cases, he continues by ensuring that the information gathered becomes a danger to and/or does not benefit the individual.

The issue here, then, is not in knowing but in converting knowledge to wisdom. In this chapter, we will discuss one lethal weapon of the devil capable of such disruption. To do this, we will look at a few examples from the Bible first, see the common denominator and shed light on how to overcome it.

Adam and Eve

We will start our studies with the first people on whom the devil played his trick. As per the scriptures, Adam and Eve were the first people God created. Genesis 1:26, *then God said, "Let Us make man in Our image, according to Our likeness; let them have dominion over the fish of the sea, over the birds of the air, and over the cattle, over all the earth and over every creeping thing that creeps on the earth.* It was the start of Adam and Eve. The goal was for them to have dominion over everything that was made. It took God six days to create, and it was on the sixth day that He formed Adam (Genesis 1:31). From God's statement in Genesis 1:27-30, we can say that everything created before the sixth day was made for man. Later, God made the woman, Eve, to be a help-mate to Adam (Genesis 2:18). Together, at the time of creation, the man and the woman were perfect specimens.

An incident then happened, in Genesis 3, that led to the fall of man. In this incident, we will deduce one lethal weapon the enemy uses to bring people down. The goal of this weapon is to ensure that the dominion promised by God is never achieved. However, before we get into this incident, let us deduce the terms of the contract/agreement God gave Adam.

Then the Lord God took the man and put him in the garden of Eden to tend and keep it. And the Lord God commanded the man, saying, "Of every tree of the garden you may freely eat; but of the tree of the knowledge of good and evil you shall not eat, for in the day that you eat of it you shall surely die." Genesis 2:15-17.

Like Adam, God has placed us on the earth with a mission. In my case, it is to bring the light of understanding into the darkness of deception by teaching the word of God. In the case of Adam, it was to tend and keep the garden. In other words, it is the main reason God made you. By tending the garden, Adam was destined to have dominion; however, there was a caveat to this. Like every contract, there are conditions. Some things will make the contract void and/or lead to legal jeopardy. Nevertheless, it was the stipulation God made in the scripture above.

I have heard people ask questions like, "why would God put this tree in the garden?" Here is the reason. We don't take every other woman away from the earth because a man enters a marriage contract. No! The man's free will to stay with his wife makes him a faithful and righteous husband. When we love someone, we give them the ability to make their own choices. Such was what God was doing here. Secondly, like an ecosystem, believe it or not, the tree of knowledge of good and evil is essential to the proper functioning of the garden. With it, the garden will function as designed. However, Adam's ability to stick with the terms of his contract will justify him before God. From here, we can see that after we have located our garden (the world, primarily as kings and/or the body of Christ, primarily as priests), we must understand our function (that is, how to tend—the five-fold offices).

The next thing to figure out from God is our tree of knowledge of good and evil. To every man, there is this tree that we must avoid. Many know their garden and what to do but are oblivious to their tree of knowledge of good and evil. From scripture, we see that death is inevitable by eating from this tree. It means that dominion becomes impossible. The quickest way to lose our place in God is to eat from this abomination tree. Since every man has a vision from God to fulfil on earth, then we all have the tree of knowledge of good and evil.

Now let us look at the incident in Genesis 3 to uncover the devil's weapon.

Now the serpent was more cunning than any beast of the field which the Lord God had made. And he said to the woman, "Has God indeed said, 'You shall not eat of every tree of the garden'? "And the woman said to the serpent, "We may eat the fruit of the trees of the garden; but of the fruit of the tree, which is in the midst of the garden, God has said, 'You shall not eat it, nor shall you touch it, lest you die.'" Then the serpent said to the woman, "You will not surely die. For God knows that in the day you eat of it your eyes will be opened, and you will be like God, knowing good and evil." So, when the woman saw that the tree was good for food, that it was pleasant to the eyes, and a tree desirable to make one wise, she took of its fruit and ate. She also gave to her husband with her, and he ate. Then the eyes of both of them were opened, and they knew that they were naked; and they sewed fig leaves together and made themselves coverings. Genesis 3:1-7.

Adam's call was to tend the garden, and Eve's to help him. However, from the scripture above, the serpent successfully shifted Eve's attention to a tree in the garden. It happened because she focused on another rather than her call. She entertained an entity that was not part of her call. In answering this entity, she shifted her focus from her call. When it comes to our call, we must always have conversations with those that are a solution or problem. Any random conversation with random entities has the potential to distract. While distracted, Eve lost focus of her assignment and made terrible decisions, including that of her assignment. Eve's focus shifted, and she lost sight of her assignment. So, instead of helping Adam avoid the forbidden fruit, she gave it to him. When we lose focus of our call through deception and/or otherwise, we make the wrong decision for our actual calling.

On the other hand, Adam lost focus of his assignment by being distracted. He focused on Eve rather than the call. There is time for everything (Ecclesiastes 3:1). Taking the fruit from Eve without objection indicated that he was still awestruck by Eve. From his statement in Genesis 2:23, we can deduce that Adam was mesmerized by Eve. He was still in this state and focused on her when he was supposed to be focused on his assignment. We only make the right decisions when we focus on our assignments. Any deviation leaves us making the wrong decision(s) as it pertains to our call.

Finally, the deduction here is that both Adam and Eve focus on something/someone else rather than their assignment. It is simply a distraction, making them dangerous to their call. Quoting my spiritual father, *"the plan of God does not change, but the people can ."* When a person becomes detrimental to their call, God replaces them quickly. It was done in this case, as seen in Genesis 3:24

So, He drove out the man; and He placed cherubim at the east of the garden of Eden, and a flaming sword which turned every way, to guard the way to the tree of life.

Father Abraham

The next case study we will examine is the father of faith, Abraham. He started well, but something happened during his journey that still affects today's world.

Like Adam, God gave a condition for everyone He called/created. These were the terms of the contract that must be focused on. Any deviation from this can have a catastrophic impact on a person's destiny. To understand the condition given to Abram, we will look at the call of Abraham.

Now the Lord had said to Abram: "Get out of your country, from your family and from your father's house to a land that I will show you. I will make you a great nation. I will bless you and make your name great; And you shall be a blessing. I will bless those who bless you, And I will curse him who curses you; And in you all the families of the earth shall be blessed." Genesis 12:1-5.

From the scripture above, Abram was given enough instruction to pursue a dominion destiny. God stipulated that coming back to Him at every turn was the term of Abram's contract. By following this path, he was on top by Genesis 13. So, the key to Abram's destiny was to focus on God. When it pertains to his destiny, God must be the one who shows him and tells him the land to dwell. Such was his equivalent of tending the garden; therefore, Abram had many encounters with God.

However, an incident happened in Genesis 16. This incident put a dent in Abram's destiny forever, simply because he decided not to follow the condition this time. Let us read the account below.

Now Sarai, Abram's wife, had borne him no children. And she had an Egyptian maidservant whose name was Hagar. So Sarai said to Abram, "See now, the Lord has restrained me from bearing children. Please, go into my maid; perhaps I shall obtain children by her." And Abram heeded the voice of Sarai. Then Sarai, Abram's wife, took Hagar her maid, the Egyptian, and gave her to her husband Abram to be his wife, after Abram had dwelt ten years in the land of Canaan. So, he went into Hagar, and she conceived. And when she saw that she had conceived, her mistress became despised in her eyes. Genesis 16:1-4.

Here is the issue: the first time God spoke to Abram, He kept some of the information back. He said, "to the land, I will show you"; this indicates that Abraham must rely on God. In this scripture above, Sarai suggested, and Abram yielded. He never thought to ask God about this suggestion. Like Adam, Abram forsook his way to the top and focused on his wife. He relies on his wife instead of his God. By paying attention to Sarai, Abram was distracted from where/what God had planned to show him. Again, this was simply a distraction.

If we read Genesis 15, we will see that God entered a covenant with Abram to affirm that he would have his heir. However, as his destiny demanded, God did not tell Abram when. Such is because relying on God was the core of Abram's dominion destiny. Due to this mishap, Abram gave birth to a son–Ishmael, who was not the promised son. This son changed the course of God's plan for Abram. Many antiChrist things today can be traced back to this mistake. Abram was not replaced because, in Genesis 17, when he was confronted and instructed by God on the issue, he humbled himself and obeyed. Unlike Adam, who tried to shift the blame. Yes, God can restore, but for every action, there are reactions–consequences.

So, for every call are conditions. We must always align with these conditions to reach the top and attain dominion.

Samson

Like Abram, Samson is another fantastic individual we can learn from. From Judges 13:4-5, the condition of Samson's dominion was quite clear. *Therefore, please be careful not to drink wine or similar drinks and not to eat anything unclean. For behold, you shall conceive and bear a son. And no razor shall come upon his head, for the child shall be a Nazirite to God from the womb; and he shall begin to deliver Israel out of the hand of the Philistines."* From these scriptures, we know that Samson's way to the top is for him to be a Nazarene to God. However, to be that, he must avoid wine or similar drinks, and no razor must come on his head. Yes, God gave these conditions to Samson's parents, but it was clear from Judges 16:17 that this instruction was communicated to Samson as well.

In the case of Samson, his hair was the forbidden fruit he must never eat. Like the tree of knowledge of good and evil, Samson paid attention to this clause for a while; thus, he was fine for as long as he did that. He was focused on his call and conditions to destroy the enemies of Israel with the help of God. However, something happened in Judges 16 that changed his life. Like Adam and Eve never recover, Samson never recovers from this mistake. Therefore, we must understand that though God is merciful and the restorer, it is always better not to fall. Let us look at the fall of Samson to gain understanding.

And the lords of the Philistines came up to her and said to her, "Entice him, and find out where his great strength lies, and by what means we may overpower him, that we may bind him to afflict him; and every one of us will give you eleven hundred pieces of silver." Judges 16:5

Like Adam in the garden, the devil approaches the woman (who happened to be Adam's weakness) and not him directly. It was the same approach used here by the devil. Samson was a reproach to the Philistines, who the devil backs. He was on top as destined by God for him. Such brought shame to the devil; therefore, he deduces a plan using the lords of the Philistines. The interpretation of the scripture above is this: *And the lords of the Philistines came up to her (Delilah) and said to her, "Distract him then you can find the source of his dominion reign."*

From the scriptures, we can deduce that Samson loves strange women. He jumps from one woman to another. In some cases, even harlots, also known as prostitutes. Though this had no direct effect on his power, it was still against the command of God for Israel. Their collective agreement with God was not to lie with strange women, particularly non-Israelites (Deuteronomy 7:3). Samson flagrantly disobeyed this. Yet, his power and dominion reign never took a hit, or so it seemed. Here is why: though something might not be a forbidden tree for us, if it is against the commands of God, we'd better drop it. Though this seemed not to affect Samson's dominion reign, it created a loophole for the enemy. What is not of God is of the devil. There is no middle ground. As such, the devil will use what is his, in and around us, to figure out our secrets, distract us, and get us to eat the forbidden fruit. Thus, we must keep ourselves clear of everything God frowns upon, and we'll shut the devil out completely (See Ephesians 4:27).

The next thing to point out here is that the lords of the Philistines, who are diabolical (Judges 16:13), didn't know the source of Samson's strength. Do not be deceived; the devil doesn't know everything. If he did, there wouldn't be a need for this trap. In 1 Corinthians 2:8, the devil had no idea that killing Jesus would bring us salvation, though God had clarified this through many prophecies. Unless we hand this information over carelessly, the devil doesn't have access to what God has said to us. So, we are to guard what God has spoken to us and keep it within the circle of God-ordained people.

And it came to pass, when she pestered him daily with her words and pressed him, so that his soul was vexed to death, that he told her all his heart, and said to her, "No razor has ever come upon my head, for I have been a Nazirite to God from my mother's womb. If I am shaven, then my strength will leave me, and I shall become weak, and be like any other man." Judges 16:16-17

Samson had been able to keep his eye on the ball for a long time while he was with strange women. However, something changed here. The devil matched his will with a stronger will—Delilah, who, with the devil's help, pestered him daily. As such, he shifted his eye from the goal to the fact that he was vexed to death. At this point, his fight or flight figuratively kicked in, and he succumbed to the pressure. Such is the danger of toying with sin and iniquities. You have a destiny to preserve, and these tools of the devil have the mandate to destroy destinies. While flirting with sin and iniquity, we are not under the protection of

God; as such, we can never outrun these deadly tools of distractions.

When Delilah saw that he had told her all his heart, she sent and called for the lords of the Philistines, saying, "Come up once more, for he has told me all his heart." So, the lords of the Philistines came up to her and brought the money in their hand. Then she lulled him to sleep on her knees and called for a man and had him shave off the seven locks of his head. Then she began to torment him, and his strength left him. And she said, "The Philistines are upon you, Samson!" So, he awoke from his sleep, and said, "I will go out as before, at other times, and shake myself free!" But he did not know that the Lord had departed from him. Then the Philistines took him and put out his eyes and brought him down to Gaza. They bound him with bronze fetters, and he became a grinder in the prison. Judges 16:18-21

In conclusion, we must understand that no matter how friendly sin or an unbeliever may be, anyone or anything not in God has allegiance only to the devil. Either parents, siblings or a friend cannot help themselves but be of service to the devil. Jesus said, *He who is not with Me is against Me, and he who does not gather with Me scatters* (Luke 11:23). When the sin Samson was toying with destroyed him, she, the sinner, was rewarded and possibly crowned hero by the devil. Beware! Samson went from the top to the absolute bottom because he gave room to the devil, who successfully distracted him.

King Saul

Another individual worth analyzing is the first king of Israel. He became a king by chance when the people of

Israel wanted to be like other nations. There was no precedence for him to follow or how to do this. But God ensured that he had someone to guide and help him through. He was ordained king in 1 Samuel 10. By 1 Samuel 12, Prophet Samuel gave clear directions and conditions for his ordination for the king and the nation of Israel. Let's look at these conditions.

"Now therefore, here is the king whom you have chosen and whom you have desired. And take note, the Lord has set a king over you. If you fear the Lord and serve Him and obey His voice, and do not rebel against the commandment of the Lord, then both you and the king who reigns over you will continue following the Lord your God. However, if you do not obey the voice of the Lord, but rebel against the commandment of the Lord, then the hand of the Lord will be against you, as it was against your fathers. 1 Samuel 12:13-15.

From these, we can deduce that the condition for their dominion is obeying the Lord's commandments. It seems simple enough, but as we have seen thus far, the tool of the devil called distraction makes us go against these conditions. In the case of King Saul, his major mistake, among many others, occurred in 1 Samuel 13:8-14. See the account below.

Then he (Saul) waited seven days, according to the time set by Samuel. But Samuel did not come to Gilgal; and the people were scattered from him. So, Saul said, "Bring a burnt offering and peace offerings here to me." And he offered the burnt offering. Now it happened, as soon as he had finished presenting the burnt offering, that Samuel came; and Saul went out to meet him, that he might greet him. And Samuel said, "What have you done?" Saul said, "When I saw that the people were scattered from me, and that you did not come within the days appointed, and that the Philistines gathered together at Michmash, then I said, 'The Philistines will now come down on me at Gilgal, and I have not made supplication to the Lord.' Therefore, I felt compelled, and offered a burnt offering." And Samuel said to Saul, "You have done foolishly. You have not kept the commandment of the Lord your God, which He commanded you. For now, the Lord would have established your kingdom over Israel forever. But now your kingdom shall not continue. The Lord has sought for Himself a man after His own heart, and the Lord has commanded him to be commander over His people, because you have not kept what the Lord commanded you."

Before diving into the scripture above, we must understand that God chose Saul because he was available. Saul was not ready for the job; God had to modify him to make him what he needed (1 Samuel 10:9). Saul never had to put in the work. God gave it to him because the people requested it, and Saul was favored. As such, Saul was under a probationary period, as seen in the statement of Samuel in 1 Samuel 13:13. We must learn from this and view every call of God on our life, even our destiny, as a probation. As quoted earlier, the plan of God does not change, but the people he uses can. Therefore, we see all assignments as probation until we depart the earth to heaven. God can "fire" us at any time if we are not following the conditions of our engagement.

As per the continuous commandment of God for Israel, only the God-ordained people can offer sacrifices to God. The King's job was to lead the governmental affairs of the people to ensure that they followed the commandments of God. As such, there is room for the Priest. The King is different from the Priest, which was clear from the law of

God throughout time in ancient Israel. By offering sacrifice, King Saul went against the clear commandment.

Since Saul was appointed King, he seemed to have a hard time completely obeying God, which is also disobedience in the sight of God. However, God was merciful until something shifted. Saul cited three reasons for his mishap. Let us analyze each for better understanding. First, Saul's kingship happened because the Lord needed someone for that post.

From Saul's statement in 1 Samuel 13:11, the first reason he gave was that he saw the people scatter from him. For him to see this implies that Saul shifted focus from being the Shepherd to the flock; he got distracted by his subjects. Such was his mistake. As King, he could have commanded the people to stay; instead, he wanted to please the people rather than God. By doing this, he was compromised and made the wrong call. Like Adam and Eve, we make bad decisions about our actual call when we focus on the wrong things and/or people.

The second reason he gave was that Samuel had yet to arrive as promised, and the Philistines gathered at Michmach. The enemy will always gather as long as we live here on earth. There will always be a reason to worry, be anxious, et al., but this only happens to us when we focus on their gathering. Saul knew that the Philistines gathered because he was focused on them. He kept tabs on them and knew exactly what was happening with them. He did this, losing sight of where God was on the case. He kept tabs on the enemy but lost sight of God's servant—Samuel. Such is not correct. Our focus should always be on God, who sent us. In Isaiah 54:15, the Bible says *indeed they shall surely assemble, but not because of Me. Whoever assembles against you shall fall for your sake.* Such affirmed that the enemy will always gather. Still, we are more than conquerors (Romans 8:37). This is possible because for God to arise and His enemies to be scattered (Psalm 68:1), they must first gather/assemble. We are instructed to be anxious for nothing (Philippians 4:6); therefore, you may keep tabs on your enemies but never lose sight of God. The enemy's vices and movement must never consume us; God and His ways must consume us, focused on pleasing God and have a healthy and not obsessed knowledge of the enemy's strategies (2 Corinthians 2:11).

The last reason Saul gave was that he did what he did because he hadn't supplicated to the LORD. It might seem like a great thing to do; however, this is what I call "good distractions," and as a result, it cost him the kingdom. His job was to Shepherd the people, not offer sacrifice to God for the people. Making supplications before the war was good, but not his job or call. Though it was a good thing, he did the right thing the wrong way, and it cost him. By leaving our post to do someone else's job, we leave our responsibilities lagging. As such, we are distracted by a good cause. No matter the good intention or the good of what we are doing, if we are not called to do it, we are distracted and will pay dearly for that distraction. God's assignment can never lag. He has a backup of backups. Don't worry about it. Just stay in your lane and focus on your responsibilities. Let God take care of other people's lags. Unless God specifically adds it to your responsibility (Matthew 25:29), it is wrong to do it. Regardless of the good.

In conclusion, Saul lost his kingdom forever by doing what wasn't his responsibility to do. Neither he nor his lineage could repair the damage caused by simply disobeying the commands of God, even though it might be, or is supposed to be, a good reason/cause. The reason for the breach is never the point as the breach itself. Saul did something foolish because he did not keep the commandment of God, which was the main thing his dominion was anchored on.

King David

Another great individual we will be looking at in our studies is King David. For every Christian today, this is a household name. David was the first King of Israel that God Himself selected and put on the throne. As per Acts 13:22, David was a man after God's heart. God made him for this, unlike Saul, who was an accidental king. However, looking through the life of David, we saw that despite all this greatness, a significant error affected his life significantly. It marred his legacy and destiny, and he paid dearly for that error. Now let us examine this mess and learn from it.

It happened in the spring of the year, at the time when kings go out to battle, that David sent Joab and his servants with him, and all Israel; and they destroyed the people of Ammon and besieged Rabbah. But David remained at Jerusalem. 2 Samuel 11:1.

The statement "at the time when kings go out to battle" shows us the condition of David's call. He was the king, and this was his responsibility; however, he chose to stay back when he should have been at war. This decision was the foundation of the catastrophe that befell David. Each time we neglect or take a break from what we ought to be doing, we are calling forth catastrophe. By this act of negligence, we are keeping doors open for destruction. There is room for delegation, but there are things that we must never delegate; these are the conditions of our calls. So, are you a king? There are wars you must always go to. Ask yourself, am I where I ought to be?

Another crucial point from this scripture is that David's delegates were doing a great job. They destroyed the people of Ammon, but their winnings did not avert trouble from David. We should take up our responsibility and lose than neglect it and win.

Then it happened one evening that David arose from his bed and walked on the roof of the king's house. And from the roof he saw a woman bathing, and the woman was very beautiful to behold. So, David sent and inquired about the woman. And someone said, "Is this not Bathsheba, the daughter of Eliam, the wife of Uriah the Hittite?" Then David sent messengers, and took her; and she came to him, and he lay with her, for she was cleansed from her impurity; and she returned to her house. And the woman conceived; so, she sent and told David, and said, "I am with child." 2 Samuel 11:2-5

We are equipped to do what we have been called to do. There is an authority given to us for what God has called us to do. David was king, and as such, there was an authority he commanded. By being in the wrong place, David exercises his God-given power and authority incorrectly. Power and authority exerted wrongly will produce negative consequences. He used his power and authority, meant for the battle then, to abuse his subject. Many leaders are in this predicament because they are in the wrong place. Power is the ability to get things done. When we have it, it drives us. Due to this fact, we are bound to get other things done when we neglect our responsibilities.

The other things, either good or bad, are distractions. We must locate the place and purpose of God's power, situating ourselves properly for the power to be beneficial. Any power used where God has not ordained it to be used is an abuse. By not being at war, David had no choice but to find a distraction where he abused power. In the same way, when a person is not where they ought to be or neglect their responsibility, they will abuse their power.

When the wife of Uriah heard that Uriah her husband was dead, she mourned for her husband. And when her mourning was over, David sent and brought her to his house, and she became his wife and bore him a son. But the thing that David had done displeased the Lord. 2 Samuel 11:26-27.

David continued in this spray of power abuse. He killed the woman's husband and took the wife. Let us put this in perspective, by staying home when he ought to be at war, he possibly raped a married woman, got her pregnant and killed the husband. Nothing like this would have happened if he had gone to war and done his responsibility. When we leave our post, we are not covered. We are exposed, and the devil can suggest things to us. One of the ways we shut the devil's voice out is by staying busy doing what God has called us to do (Proverbs 22:29). Just like the famous saying, "an idle mind is the devil's workshop." A man of God once said an idle person is tempting the devil. Be diligent in your lane; you will never have time to ruminate on evil. By getting lost in our responsibilities, we shut the devil out. At the end of this all, God was very displeased with a man after his heart.

Then the Lord sent Nathan to David. And he came to him and said to him: "There were two men in one city, one rich and the other poor. The rich man had exceedingly many flocks and herds. But the poor man had nothing, except one little ewe lamb which he had bought and nourished; and it grew up together with him and with his children. It ate of his own food and drank from his own cup and lay in his bosom; and it was like a daughter to him. And a traveler came to the rich man, who refused to take from his own flock and from his own herd to prepare one for the wayfaring man who had come to him; but he took the poor man's lamb and prepared it for the man who had come to him." So, David's anger was greatly aroused against the man, and he said to Nathan, "As the Lord lives, the man who has done this shall surely die! And he shall restore fourfold for the lamb, because he did this thing and because he had no pity." Then Nathan said to David, "You are the man! Thus says the Lord God of Israel: 'I anointed you king over Israel, and I delivered you from the hand of Saul. I gave you your master's house and your master's wives into your keeping and gave you the house of Israel and Judah. And if that had been too little, I also would have given you much more! Why have you despised the commandment of the Lord, to do evil in His sight? You have killed Uriah the Hittite with the sword; you have taken his wife to be your wife and have killed him with the sword of the people of Ammon. Now therefore, the sword shall never depart from your house, because you have despised Me, and have taken the wife of Uriah the Hittite to be your wife.' Thus says the Lord: 'Behold, I will raise up adversity against you from your own house; and I will take your wives before your eyes and give them to your neighbor, and he shall lie with your wives in the sight of this sun. For you did it secretly, but I will do this thing before all Israel before the sun.'" So, David said to Nathan, "I have sinned against the Lord. "And Nathan said to David, "The Lord also has put away your sin; you shall not die. However, because by this deed you have given great occasion to the enemies of the Lord to blaspheme, the *child also who is born to you shall surely die." Then Nathan departed to his house.* 2 Samuel 12:1-15.

In Luke 12:48, we know what God expects from each of us is synonymous with who He has made us and what He has made available to us. Moses missed the promised land by virtue of who he was. David, being a king, has power and authority. He had the opportunity to ask God for more wealth, women etc., and God would have answered him. Due to this fact, this error carries higher consequences. From the scripture above, we saw that David brought curses into his home by simply neglecting his post and abusing his power. The curse of the sword and adversity in his house came to pass when David's son, Absalom, killed Amon, his half-brother, for raping Tamar, his sister (2 Samuel 13). In addition, we saw David in his old age, running from Absalom, who was bent on killing him (2 Samuel 15), and Absalom raping David's concubines in public (2 Samuel 16:21-22). The son conceived by Bathsheba did not survive.

Despite David's repentance, the consequences of his action came to pass. God forgave him, but the implications of this error stayed with him throughout his life and even afterwards. He lost Amnon, Absalom, and the son conceived by Bathsheba. He also opened the door to the devil to have free flow in his family, from incest to letting all kinds of evil exist in his house, simply because he neglected his post and was distracted. We must understand that God is merciful, so he will always forgive; however, for every action, there are reactions–consequences. Borrowing my spiritual father's quote, the sin issue is never forgiveness; it is restoring what we've lost because of sin. Due to this negligence, David was never the same again; thus, it is better not to fall than to fall and get healed. The scar will be there forever.

In conclusion, David was distracted because he was positioned where he ought not to be. It is simply impossible to be distracted when we are where God wants us to be. Always locate the place and remain there. Distraction will be impossible when you are always conscious of your physical and figurative location. We become distracted when we are in the wrong place at any point in time. The force of the power in us wants to express itself; hence, we can become distracted looking for where to espouse this power.

Judas

The next person we will examine is Judas Iscariot. He was a man who had one of the greatest privileges anyone could be afforded on earth in the flesh. Jesus, God in the flesh, came down to this world and chose him as one of the apostles. What a privilege! As per Luke 6:12-14, we saw that Judas was selected by Jesus prayerfully. The nature and the amount of prayer that Jesus put in before He appointed him suggests a great vision ahead of him. Judas was destined for a great thing. God had a fantastic future ahead of him. To put this in perspective, many were alive at his time, yet Judas was chosen as one of the disciples. There were many disciples, yet Judas was selected as one of the twelve apostles. Although many of us today serve God through proxies, Judas had the privilege of serving alongside Jesus. Such privileges, among many other things, were the privileges that God afforded Judas. But somehow, he ended up a brand name for traitors.

How could this happen? To be clear, every one of Jesus' disciples were imperfect people. In fact, from Mark 2:17, it is evident that they were sinners, in other words, sick people. So, Judas was not the only imperfect person chosen by Jesus. But, it was the perfect case of what God does. He calls the unqualified to qualify them for the job. He chose sick people so that he could heal them. So, God intended to cure, equip, train, and wash them; however, we are beings of free will. Like everyone, God *will set before us life and good, death and evil* (Deuteronomy 30:15); He will urge us to choose life, but the choice is ours. God did the same thing for the disciples; therefore, we had many other disciples turn out as ones we look up to, such as Peter, James, and John. Judas ended up being one we never want to be like; he became a household name for traitors. To be very clear, Judas was never called to be the traitor; he chose to be that. God never calls anyone to meet a quota. Everyone will decide what kind of vessel they want to be (2 timothy 2:20-21).

Judas had all the opportunities the others had, but his sickness made him vulnerable. The devil was able to use it to gain access because of it. Something he never realized was an issue until it led him to his death. This thing is the strategy of the devil we want to uncover. Let us read from the scriptures to gain more insight.

Then, six days before the Passover, Jesus came to Bethany, where Lazarus was who had been dead, whom He had raised from the dead. There they made Him a supper; and Martha served, but Lazarus was one of those who sat at the table with Him. Then Mary took a pound of very costly oil of spikenard, anointed the feet of Jesus, and wiped His feet with her hair. And the house was filled with the fragrance of the oil. But one of His disciples, Judas Iscariot, Simon's son, who would betray Him, said, "Why was this fragrant oil not sold for three hundred denarii and given to the poor?" This he said, not that he cared for the poor, but because he was a thief, and had the money box; and he used to take what was put in it. John 12:1-6.

From the scripture above, we saw that there was a desire in Judas that the devil was able to exploit. Here is the fact; we all have one or more weaknesses. The Bible, in Galatians 5:19-21, listed the works of the flesh; these are the weaknesses. For as long as we are in the flesh, the flesh has one or more of these works. For Judas, it was greed and covetousness. If this was the case, and Jesus being God knew this, why did Judas have the money box? As mentioned earlier, God called and gave us responsibilities, not because we are qualified, but because He wants to qualify us for that responsibility. In other words, we are not qualified for God's call. We are chosen by grace. This way, we can depend on him to train us and, in that same vein, remain humble. Judas had the money box precisely because of his weakness. Remember, God cannot heal us until we know we are sick (Matthew 7:7-8). So, often God may put us in a situation that will reveal our sickness. It is so we can know our issue and approach Him for help. Judas was given the money box to see his sickness and ask Jesus for help. Instead, he concealed it and fulfilled Proverbs 28:13 in the process. Thus, we can let God use our weakness to grow us or allow the devil to use it to destroy us.

God and the devil know this weakness; however, God is bringing it to our attention not to condemn us but to get us to seek help. Therefore, we are convicted as we exhibit the works of the flesh. On the other hand, the devil sees it as an opportunity to steal, kill and destroy. Due to the two different results, God ensures that these things are concealed in our call and that the help we need is abundant. By keeping the money box, Judas was serving God and, at the same time, was shown his area of weakness. Jesus was available to ensure the sickness was healed and perfected if he asked for help. The devil, on the other hand, saw an opportunity to exploit. He will make this the only thing a person sees and how "beneficial" it may be in the meantime. Judas was so consumed by it that he now sees everything from the lens of his weakness. So, the moment our focus shifts from our assignment to our weakness, or the weakness that the assignment may expose, this indicates that the devil is exploiting us. Therefore, we must be on guard not to give the devil a foothold (Ephesians 4:27). When the assignment exposes our flaws, we must run to God for help because He has already made provision for it. You won't be exposed to a condition if there is yet to be a provision.

In Luke 22, we see that it was this greed that the enemy used on Judas to betray Jesus. Judas later realized what he had done, and instead of repenting, the spirit of condemnation persuaded him to kill himself (Matthew 27).

In conclusion, Judas was a rising star who died untimely because his attention shifted from his call to the weakness exposed by the call. It was the tactics of the devil. What we focus on is what we eventually become attracted to. When we stare at our weakness long enough, we fall in love with it, and this becomes a distraction. We look at everything, including our call, from this lens. Remember, assignments from God have the potential to expose our weaknesses; however, the intention is for us to seek God for the abundance of help He has made available. We saw many instances in the scriptures where situations exposed Apostle Peter's weaknesses, but he always ran back to God for healing. Such must always be the approach. Do not fantasize about the weaknesses; instead, like a sick person, go to God for both the diagnosis and healing.

The Device: Distractions

From the people we have looked at, we can see a common theme, they were distracted before the devil destroyed them. From Adam and Eve to Judas, their focus was shifted, or they misused time before the devil could steal, kill and destroy.

Let us start by debunking a myth. From the creation of man, we saw that God breathed into man, and he became a living being (Genesis 2:7). To stay alive, we need the breath of God. Since this is the breath of God, it, therefore, belongs to God. Due to this, there is a longing for God in every human (Ecclesiastes 3:11); therefore, from time immemorial, humans have always longed to connect with the supernatural in many ways. Unfortunately, only some did it right, while others needed to be corrected. But for as long as we are alive, we will never be complete until we belong to the only true God (John 17:3). Matthew 6:33 says to *seek first the kingdom of God and His righteousness, and all these things shall be added to you.* So, we see that if humans are to stay alive, complete and live without chaos in our being, attention to one thing (the only true God) is not a suggestion but a necessity.

Hear this, to excel in anything; multitasking is a fallacy. We will discuss this deeper shortly. It is impossible to serve God and mammon at the same time. You will honor one and despise the other (Matthew 6:24). The mammon here symbolizes everything and anything parallel to God and will never cross paths. Therefore, due to the criticality of focusing on God, the devil devises a condition that affects the physical and spiritual to ensure that humans are never complete for as long as they are alive. At the same time, the devil steals, kills, and destroys.

As you read the previous paragraph, you might be thinking, but I know people who didn't focus on God at all; in fact, some may be atheists or agnostics, yet they seem to have a great life, better than some children of God. I will start by saying all through the scriptures, God never said that we would not get results outside of Him. As we have established in this book, the gift of God is for everyone; however, He made it clear that we will never be complete without Him. Remember, we are and remain alive because of His breath, so for as long as we are alive, His breath in us will always long for Him. It creates an eternal hole in us that God can only fill. In Deuteronomy 30:19, He set before the Israelite life and death and urged them to choose life. In Matthew 6:24, He placed God and mammon before us; in Matthew 6:33, He told us a way to make mammon serve us; therefore, it is our choice. Thus, we can see that those who chose mammon may still generate results. In addition, since multitasking is an enemy of excellence, we will excel at whatever we give our attention to and yield results. Only focusing on God can deliver overall results (Matthew 6:33 & John 10:10). Another aspect worth looking at is the time factor here. For anything to yield results, time is needed. For whatever option we choose, we must invest time to see it yield; therefore, some that chose mammon might seem to have a better life than some children of God due to time investment (Ecclesiastes 9:11). It is in these two that the devil has perfected his craft of distraction. Now let us dive deeper.

THE PATH TO DOMINION

Do you see a man who excels in his work? He will stand before kings; He will not stand before unknown men. Proverbs 22:29.

Whatever your hand finds to do, do it with you might; for there is no work or device or knowledge or wisdom in the grave where you are going. I returned and saw under the sun that— The race is not to the swift, Nor the battle to the strong, nor bread to the wise, nor riches to men of understanding, nor favor to men of skill; But time and chance happen to them all. Ecclesiastes 9:10-11

From Proverbs 22:29, we see that to stand before kings, symbolizing dominion, we must first excel in our work. Therefore, it is excelling in our works that yield dominion results. Ecclesiastes 9:10-11 shows us the path to excel. First, we must do *whatever our hand finds to do with our might* (Ecclesiastes 9:10), and secondly, continue until time and chance come (Ecclesiastes 9:11). So, whatever we focus on and not lose hope on, must yield excellent results in that regard. Let us take each path to excellence and see how the devil can use distraction to thwart the dominion goal.

Focus

There is a simple definition of distraction from the Merriam-Webster dictionary. It states that distraction is any object that directs one's attention away from something else. It connotes a loss of focus. We must understand that for anything to produce results; we must give it our full attention; hence, the command of the scripture in Ecclesiastes 9:10.

We see the devil's mission in John 10:10. *The thief does not come except to steal, kill, and destroy.* Every successful influence of the devil starts with stealing; however, the devil can only steal after we are successfully distracted. Today, the devil seemed to have accumulated much power because of his ability to distract; therefore, whenever we lose focus, we lose something as the devil steals from us.

Once we figure out our call, we must locate the works/efforts and do it with our might. It is in this realm that skill and sturdiness are developed. To excel in our work means to be the best at what we do. For this reason, skills are needed. We saw the criticality of skills when the Bible said in Psalm 78:72 that David *shepherded them according to the integrity of his heart and guided them by the skillfulness of his hands.* Though David was a man after God's own heart (Acts 13:22), this did not replace the necessity for needed skills. There is no spiritual substitute for skills; however, we can ask God for speed while developing the skills. No matter what God has called us to do, there are earthly skills required, and we must focus on acquiring, improving and/or building them. Such is what focus presents us with.

Previously, we established that to have all-round success and completeness in life; we must focus on God alone. In doing so, He then takes care of the other things that need our attention (See Matthew 6:33), but here we are saying to focus on our work/effort to grow in the skills required. The question then becomes, which one is it? When these two are done right, they are the same; therefore, focusing on God for you and me may mean different things depending on the call.

To focus on God alone, we must come to God through Jesus as commanded in Romans 10:9-10; after which we locate our mini destinies/callings, using some or all the methods listed in this book. Once this is done, we must stay in our lane, as stated in chapter 3, and focus. We are focusing on God alone by letting God lead us in the 5Ws (who, what, where, when and why) and 1H (how) of our calling. By letting God be the alpha and the omega of our calling, we are focusing on Him alone. Whether our calling is mainly in the kingship or priesthood realm, we bring it all under God, and He is the core and main factor. Such is how we make God the focus through His calling on our life. Due to this fact, the devil has a tool he uses to shift our focus.

Multitasking

There is a device that the devil has seemed to perfect to thwart our focus. It is called multitasking. Today in the world, this is a great thing, especially in the secular work circle. Some companies base their requirement on this so-called great skill; however, as we will see here, it is a tactic of the devil to stop a person from excelling, making dominion impossible.

Let's start our analysis with a simple definition of multitasking; it occurs when a person tries to do more than one thing simultaneously. From our discussion thus far, we can see how this is a problem. We have established that to excel, focus on one thing is required. So, by trying to do more than one thing, we see that excellence is impossible. If the goal is below excellence, then that is fine, but as per the scriptures, dominion requires excellence and to excel, we must focus on that thing, putting in all our might. Multitasking denies our call the fullness of our might. We are bound to share our resources, leaving us with below-excellence results. It is not a surprise as the friendship with the world is enmity to God (James 4:4); therefore, whatever the world hype will most likely be a poison for those in God.

Divided attention, aka multi-tasking, leaves a person void of skills needed to excel. The top, the dominion equivalent in the school system, is at the doctorate level. No wonder, at this stage, the field of study is very narrow. Today, there is something called attention deficit hyperactivity disorder (ADHD). It is a medical condition that affects a person's ability to be attentive and sit still (focus). It can spill out to physical activities that can render a person doing many things but achieving nothing. The equivalent of this when it comes to our destiny is multitasking. People who suffer from these demonic vices may be good at many things but are never excellent at anything nor attain dominion. Though the world sees ADHD as an issue, it considers multitasking a good thing. Spiritually, these two things thwart a person from achieving dominion, but yes, you can get multiple things done (not excellently) with multitasking. Naturally, we cannot excel in various things; hence, the command of God in Matthew 6:33. Focuses on one thing: God, and He will take care of the other things. Remember, even those with multi talents tend to be excellent at one and good at others. For example, musicians who play multiple instruments tend to have a primary instrument they excel at. Such is the fact of life that we have been blinded to by the devil.

I equate ADHD and multitasking in matters of destiny, not as an expert or a psychologist, but rather because these two attack a person's ability to focus on one thing, thereby leaving a person with a life void of dominion. God made us for dominion, so anything below this is unacceptable, and these two vices help the enemy achieve his goal.

Here is a fact, we are fascinating beings made in God's image; therefore, we will see many good things or just things we can do because *I can do all things through Christ who strengthens me* (Philippians 4:13). However, we must never forget that though *all things are lawful for me, but not all things are helpful; all things are lawful for me, but not all things edify* (1 Corinthians 10:23). The fact that we can doesn't equate to we should.

To walk with God, we must be patient. It implies that we might find ourselves in a situation like Joseph's where it seems like we are forgotten or stuck in a loop for a long time. Sometimes, until the skills are developed, we may not be allowed by God to move on. In other cases, excelling in one thing opens the door to another. So, today we focus on one thing, and as we excel, God may give us another thing to focus on, but at every point in time, there is a thing God wants all our attention on. As we will see in the next section, there is a time appointed for everything, and since God created time, He is the only Being that exists outside of time. Therefore, it makes Him the only One capable of being the custodian of time.

Finally, suppose we find ourselves multitasking and/or suffering from ADHD with matters of our destiny. In that case, we must seek God for help. It is because at the root of any loss of focus is the devil aiming to steal, kill and destroy.

Time And Chance

The next factors on the path to dominion are time and chance. To analyze this, we'd need a better look at what each of these means and then deduce from scripture how each applies.

Time

YourDictionary.com defines time as *the duration in which all things happen or a precise instant that something happens*. It is a measuring factor for happenings. It means that there is a factor of time for everything that has and will occur. For example, the earth was created at a point in time, and so were humans; even Jesus was born at a point in time. In the same way, the earth will cease to exist at some point in time. That we don't know the time has no bearing on this fact.

Diving into the scriptures, we can see that time is a factor we cannot neglect for as long as we are alive. In Ecclesiastes 3:1, the Bible says that *to everything, there is a season, A time for every purpose under the heaven*. The Aramaic translation of the Bible translated under heaven as under the sun. Fast forward to Ecclesiastes 9:11, we saw something very telling that corroborates this under-the-sun time factor. The Bible says *I returned and saw under the sun that— The race is not to the swift, nor the battle to the strong, nor bread to the wise, nor riches to men of understanding, nor favor to men of skill; But time and chance happen to them all*. It was confirmed again in Genesis 8:22, when the Bible says *while the earth remains, seedtime and harvest, cold and heat, winter and summer, and day and night shall not cease*.

So, as long as we are under the sun and on earth, time will not cease, and its influence on us will remain.

Let us expand on what we just read. The book of Ecclesiastes was believed to be written by the wisest man besides Jesus that ever lived, King Solomon. From his analysis, he realized that the race to dominion, to the top under the sun, is not just about being swift (that is shrewd, smart), strong (has physical or spiritual power and/or authority), or wisdom or wealth or skills. Though all these are needed for dominion, they all depend on the factor of time and chance to produce results. Such was why my spiritual father said by the Spirit of God, *"for anointed people, there is an appointed time."* He expounds on this line of thought using Matthew 1:17, where the word says *all the generations from Abraham to David are fourteen generations, from David until the captivity in Babylon are fourteen generations, and from the captivity in Babylon until the Christ are fourteen generations.* Though Jesus is God, He had to wait for these sets of fourteen generations to pass before He could be born. Therefore, it was His appointed time to be born; therefore, the prophetic is an office with the grasp and understanding of times. They have the unique ability to go to the future and past, then articulate in the present what they see.

For as long as we are under the sun, that is, alive physically, time is a factor that we must pay attention to. The sons of Issachar were few, yet the whole nation of Israel listened to them because they knew the times and season (1 Chronicles 12:32). Despite God being with Joseph, his journey started at the age of 17 (Genesis 37), but he never attained dominion until he the appointed age of thirty (Genesis 41). It took him 13 years of focusing on God (Genesis 39:9) to attain his dominion. For some, it might be shorter

(King Saul), and for others, longer (King David); therefore, comparison, which leads to envy and jealousy among children of God, like every tactic of the devil, is absurd. Run from it as fast as you can (James 3:16) before it destroys you, and *do not give the devil a foothold* (Ephesians 4:27).

Another point to note here is that according to Proverbs 4:18, *the path of the just is like the shining sun, that shines ever brighter unto the perfect day.* Though this may sound contradictory, we may translate this as we should be moving from glory to glory daily. While this is the correct translation, it also says we keep moving until the perfect day, which is the appointed time. Therefore, until the appointed time, what may seem like downtime is a sowing time. A time to plant first and then harvest will follow (Ecclesiastes 3:2). The path is becoming brighter, and the seed is germinating as each day goes by. So, we must always succumb to God to tell us the season we are going through. Joseph was in slavery first and then in prison. Yet, God was with Him (Genesis 39).

As we develop our skills through focus, we must understand that we are under the sun, and time is a factor. It is synonymous with the earth and spreads to everything on the earth. To be the best at anything here on earth, time for investment is needed, followed by chance. As children of God, we know we are on the right track to dominion when we enjoy God's presence through this time of planting. It is easy to see God during harvest, but we need discipline and fellowship to see God during planting.

Finally, Genesis 1:1 clearly shows that God made the heavens and the earth. Since time is an earthly phenomenon, Psalm 24:1 makes us understand that the earth and everything in it belong to the Lord; this includes time.

Therefore, we can see that God, who made the earth, created time, and He cannot be confined in time like us, and as we have examined earlier, God has put the earth in the care of the Lord, Psalm 24. As such, the Lord is the only one qualified to oversee time. So, to avoid constantly running blind, wisdom dictates a relationship with the Lord, as per Romans 10:9-10; hence, the instructions of Proverbs 3:5-6.

Trust in the LORD with all your heart and lean not on your own understanding; In all your ways acknowledge Him, and He shall direct your paths.

Obsessing Over the Past

One way the devil influences time is a distraction, obsessing over the past. As I write this, I am going through a season of planting on a particular issue. The Lord explained something to me during my meditation just before I wrote this section. I asked Lord, why is this happening? And when is this going to end? He replied, saying, that is the wrong question. I said Lord, what then is the right question? He said the right question is, how do I stand till the end? Ask for the grace to remain on top at the end (Matthew 24:13).

Brothers and Sisters, as we have explained earlier, we need to understand that whatever has a start date on earth must have an end date; however, it is those who endure to the end that will be saved (Matthew 24:13). Proverbs 24:10 says, *if we fail in the day of adversity then our strength is weak.* Such implies that during this planting season, anyone not prepared will fail. Remember, the five foolish virgins in Matthew 25 started the journey but never made it to the end. They lost out because they were unprepared.

Here was my deduction from what the Lord said; what has happened has happened. Now, what is the way forward should always be the goal. The devil comes in to get us to obsess about what already happened. When we do this, we become distracted and lose focus on staying on our feet till the end. While distracted, he can then come to steal, kill, and destroy. So, once we find ourselves in what seems like downtime and have done all we can and should, instead of asking God, why me? Or when will this ordeal end? Say, Lord, how can I stand till the end? Asking the right question is vital if we are going to walk with God. Let's think about something: depression, discouragement, offence, etc., and all the critical things people struggle with are often a product of obsessing over the past. Because of what happened in the past (maybe even repeatedly), an individual under the influence of the devil may decide to take their own life by obsessing over it. In this case, while they were obsessing over the past, the devil came and stole their joy, killed them, and destroyed them in hell.

However, to overcome this distraction, we must understand a few things. First, *God is not a man, that He should lie* Numbers 23:19. Paul the Apostle corroborated this in Romans 3:4 when He said let God be true and all men liars. Whatever our circumstances, what God has spoken to us, personally or through the scripture, will come to pass. For example, in Isaiah 3:10, He said *to the righteous (You. 2 Corinthians 5:21) that it shall be well with you, for you shall eat the fruit of your doings.* Secondly, God cannot stand or do evil. *You are of purer eyes than to behold evil* Habakkuk 1:13. God had to outsource the evil that happened to Job (Job 1:12). When His only Son (John 3:16) was carrying the evil of the whole world on the cross, God looked away from

His Son for the first and only time (Matthew 27:46). When so-called evil happens to us, don't ever allow any thoughts and/or ideas that want to blame God. He is never part of evil. Instead, ask, say, Lord, is this planting process? If so, what should I be planting? How do I endure till the end? Otherwise, rebuke that demon in the name of Jesus (Mark 16:17) and move on. But don't entertain anything that blames God for evil. Instead, let Philippians 4:8 be what filters everything about your case. Let God be the interpreter of your circumstances. Lastly, *all things work together for good to those who love God, to those who are the called according to His purpose* Romans 8:28. If you are a lover of God and trying your best to please Him, relax, the circumstances and the length of time will work for your good. Despite the length of time and every evil the devil threw at Job, he ended up with double what he started with (Before-Job 1:3, after-Job 42:12). His end was indeed great.

Chance

Per the scriptures, chance is the next thing on the path of dominion. Let us start our discussion with a simple definition. I will define chance as a time when everything aligns in our favor. We must understand that time is continuous, but chances come in cycles. For example, every day has 24 hours, but it doesn't rain every day. In this example, time is a 24-hour loop, and the chance will be the rain; therefore, we hear a forecast like this: there is a 24% chance of rain today. Chance is enveloped within time, but we must be able to discern chance to take advantage of it.

For everyone under the sun, those confined within time, there is a chance designed for us. However, if we miss the opportunity, that is the point in time when everything aligns, we may have to wait for another season. Though this is the pattern, we may lose some chances forever if we are not discerning to seize them. An example of such is this, everyone on earth only has the opportunity to be a certain age once. That is, you can only be 24 years old at one time. The chance of that happening again is zero. So, if we must do something at this age and miss it, we can't get that age back once we pass it. You can only have 2021 once; if we miss what we ought to do in 2021, we can't ever do it in 2021 again. Therefore, though time is repetitive, chances may not be.

To expound further, we will look at a man God helped to seize the chance and benefit from it. In Genesis 41:1, we saw the application of time and chance. Let us examine it closer.

Then it came to pass, at the end of two full years, that Pharaoh had a dream; and behold, he stood by the river.

The end of two years was an indication of time. It was after the accumulation of time that this chance presented itself. Chances appear after time accumulation; therefore, we must understand the relationship between time and chance. There is no chance without the accumulation of time. Thus, the accumulation of time is in the domain of the custodian of time.

Then the chief butler spoke to Pharaoh, saying: "I remember my faults this day. When Pharaoh was angry with his servants, and put me in custody in the house of the captain of the guard, both me and the chief baker, we each had a dream in one night, he and I. Each of us dreamed according to the interpretation of his own dream. Now there was a young Hebrew man with us there, a servant of the captain of the guard. And we told him, and he interpreted our dreams for us; to each man he interpreted according to his own dream. And it came to pass, just as he interpreted for us, so it happened. He restored me to my office, and he hanged him." Genesis 41:9-13

From Genesis 40, we can say that Joseph had spent time interpreting dreams for the better part of the two years. So, he had perfected this skill. When this chance presented itself, he was ready. Unlike Daniel (Daniel 2:19), Joseph never had to go to sleep to interpret Pharaoh's dream. Yes, the circumstances may be different, but the fact was that Joseph was skilled in dream interpretation. What we do with the repetition of time we had before the chance will determine what we do with the chance. The chief butler thought he was bad for forgetting Joseph for two years, but telling Pharoah about Joseph before this chance will be useless. Before now, Pharaoh had enough interpreters, and they were all doing well. God presented two years to Joseph to perfect his craft. So, as I mentioned earlier, use your planting time to focus and master your craft.

Then Pharaoh sent and called Joseph, and they brought him quickly out of the dungeon; and he shaved, changed his clothing, and came to Pharaoh. And Pharaoh said to Joseph, "I have had a dream, and there is no one who can interpret it. But I have heard it said of you that you can understand a dream, to interpret it." Genesis 41:14-15.

Here was Joseph's chance. Everything aligns for his skill. He was the only one qualified to interpret this dream. No one in the nation was better than him at what he did. It was an indication of a time well spent. He was a man in prison, yet he could focus and perfect his craft. Your current circumstance is the best place for you to perfect your craft.

Instead of complaining, settle down, focus, and utilize the time given to you. Joseph never gets another time from here, like the last few years in prison. Remember, those who use their time well take advantage of the chances.

Lack of Confidence

What the devil uses to distract here is simply a lack of confidence. It comes in the form of doubts and rationalization. Doubts come because of our fallen nature; it leaves us unsure and uncertain. It makes us unstable; and, as such, untrustworthy to receive from God (James 1:8-9), and we disqualify ourselves from the chance. Rationalization is a logical way of thinking. It seems to justify everything before steps are taken; hence, it can be deemed wisdom when it is not. It is, in fact, a lack of trust and faith in God. There is time for everything, and when the chance comes, and God says move, it is not the time to be unsure, uncertain or analyze. The devil's goal is to paralyze a person while he steals the chance.

"Now therefore, let Pharaoh select a discerning and wise man, and set him over the land of Egypt. Let Pharaoh do this, and let him appoint officers over the land, to collect one-fifth of the produce of the land of Egypt in the seven plentiful years. And let them gather all the food of those good years that are coming, and store up grain under the authority of Pharaoh, and let them keep food in the cities. Then that food shall be as a reserve for the land for the seven years of famine which shall be in the land of Egypt, that the land may not perish during the famine." Genesis 41:33-36

It is here the devil steps in and distracts many children of God. After interpreting the dream, Joseph did not stop there. No, he gave advice under the influence of the Spirit of God. It was what shot him up to dominion (See Genesis 41:37-46). It is one thing to know that this is the chance. It is another to seize that chance to our advantage. There is only one sure way to do this: by the Spirit of God. If Joseph had just interpreted, there is a possibility that he would have squandered this chance. Since God is the custodian of time, only He can bring about chances. Without Him, we stand a significant chance of squandering that chance. Those who didn't know God, who ended up taking advantage of the chance, did this because of God's mercy. No one can excel in life without the mercies of God. Therefore, as children of God, we must let Him lead us to take advantage of chances.

Joseph interpreted the dream by the Spirit of God and saw a problem. The same Spirit gave Him a solution that led to his rising. Whenever our attention is drawn to a problem, don't just blurt it out; seek God for the solution. There may lie our chance to dominion. If you can see it by the grace of God, the same grace is available to fix it. There is not a single problem in life without a solution. If we are children of God and He is pointing our attention to a problem, chances are He is willing to give us an answer. Remember, as per my spiritual father, the plan of God does not change, but the people can.

If Joseph, through doubt, had talked himself out of this solution presentation, he would have been rewarded for the interpretation, but he would not have attained dominion. It is what the devil does. We hear God give solutions, but the devil distracts us with doubt or rationalization. Through doubt and/or rationalization, we squander the chance (James 1:8). When we become unstable through doubt and waste time through rationalization, we give room to the devil, who then steals the chance from us; hence why, these are distractions. Remember, God's chances are for dominion, which the enemy doesn't want us to have. It is better to be wrong while we think we obey God than to be right while disobeying Him. If we fail in this regard, God would have to give that solution and the chance to another. Everything under the sun is timed. It implies that there is also time for every solution. If children of God fail to listen, God may be compelled to use an unbeliever or animal (Numbers 22:28).

In conclusion, we take advantage of chances by yielding to God. Therefore, it is our willingness to focus during planting (time) and absolute obedience to God during harvest (chance) that set us on high (dominion). *If you are willing and obedient, you shall eat the good of the land.* Isaiah 1:19.

GOOD AND BAD DISTRACTIONS

As we have established, the devil's goal is to restrict us from attaining dominion; therefore, his attacks are targeted toward the paths to dominion.

Distractions are simply things that take our focus and time away from what we ought to be doing. We can deduce from the definition that the good a cause may achieve doesn't matter. It is not worth our focus and time if it doesn't align with our call. One of the reasons we fall for distractions is that sometimes it may come as a good cause (2 Corinthians 11:14). We look at the good cause and think that because it is good, we must do it. It is a lie of the devil. We are only equipped for our calling. If a cause is truly good, then there are people God has called for it. Seek such people out and hand it over to them. Let us analyze this from the lens of each distraction tool.

Multitasking

Here, the enemy brings multiple visions to a person to cause distractions. It may sometimes lead to confusion where the enemy can steal the vision altogether. The bedrock of dominion is excellence. Some distractions are pure evil to our visions. These are easy to locate; however, others are justified to do. We see these things as such because they are morally right. These are the good distractions that we must also avoid. Though it may look as if it is not affecting our true calling in any way, we are taking attention away from our vision by giving it our attention. Less attention may therefore prolong the time needed to perfect our craft, and until our craft is perfected, we may squander chances. Thus, God may allow confinement (prison) for refinement, like Joseph. Do not give attention to anything because it is right, but do so because it aligns with God's vision for your life. It is how we stay in our lane and perfect our craft. When we cross lanes, we are a candidate for disqualification.

Obsessing over the Past

The past is filled with both good and evil. The goal is to get people to focus on things that have already happened while the devil steals the presence and the future. In Philippians 3:13-14, Paul the Apostle said, *I do not count myself to have apprehended; but one thing I do, forgetting those things which are behind and reaching forward to those things which are ahead, I press toward the goal for the prize of the upward call of God in Christ Jesus.* We must learn to leave the past in the past so we can focus on the future. Prophecies affirm that God is the God of the future. In Isaiah 46:10, God declares the end from the beginning. Such implies that He is already in the future waiting for you. Your future is always better than your past (Isaiah 3:10, 1 Corinthians 2:9).

When we obsess over the past, it stops us from moving forward. Looking at the bad things of the past gives the devil room to steal the future. He uses the bad of the past to define our future and stop dominion by repeating the mediocrity of the past. Such is an example of bad distractions. By looking at the good of the past, we are restricted from being better than that. We have set a bar for ourselves and don't move past it. It is an example of good distractions. In both cases, growth is thwarted, and we cannot achieve dominion. The only reason to visit the bad of the past is to learn. Once we go through the course of the past and have learned and passed the class, don't revisit it again. We visit the good of the past to thank God and create a foundation to build. This way, our latter is always better than the former (Haggai 2:9), and we are not reinventing the wheel all the time.

Lack of Confidence

It happens when we bring the flesh into the realm of the spirit. It may seem like a reasonable thing to do, but it is a display of doubt, which is simply a distraction. It is a bad distraction when we doubt based on fear, anxiety, and our inadequacies (Zachariah 4:6). It is a good distraction when we have a logical basis, such as facts, or past valid experiences, to back up our doubts (1 Corinthians 1:20 & 27). Again, this might seem wise, good, and reasonable, but it is a distraction while the devil steals from us.

In summary, the devil's goal is to steal, kill and destroy. He starts this operation through distraction. Once we are distracted by the good or the bad, he swoops in to steal. If we don't wake up, it progresses to kill, and he doesn't stop until he destroys. Therefore, when we see distractions, that is, anything competing with our focus, time, and chance, there is something valuable that must be guarded. We must rely on the Holy Spirit so the devil doesn't take advantage of us.

Chapter 5

Conclusion

As we wind down our studies, there are a few facts to life we must know and understand if we are to attain dominion.

First, God made us, and He predestined us; therefore, in Jeremiah 1:5, He was able to say *before I formed you in the womb, I knew you; Before you were born, I sanctified you; I ordained you a prophet to the nations.* In the same way, before Adam was made, God knew and predestined him (Genesis 1:26). So was Eve (Genesis 2:18). Therefore, before you and I were created, God knew us and predestined us as well. It was corroborated in Amos 3:7, where the Bible says *the Lord GOD does nothing unless He reveals His secret to His servants, the prophets.* Therefore, before our birth, God must have spoken about us. At least a servant of God knew about our existence before we existed. Thus, it is impossible to attain the height God has for us if we don't know what was said about us. It is in this that His predestination for us lies. Approaching our Maker is the first step to uncovering our predestination and owning our destiny. We cannot attain dominion unless we go through the sovereign of all.

We do this through Jesus (See John 10:10 and Romans 10:9-10).

Secondly, the Bible made us understand that *whoever wants to be a friend of the world makes himself an enemy of God.* (James 4:4); therefore, you cannot serve two masters (Matthew 6:24). Contrary to the devil's delusion, humans have no middle ground in life. Our free will is choosing between God and the devil, good and evil, slave to righteousness or slave to sin, etc. The thought and the impression of a middle ground is simply a tactic of the devil to lead us to disobedience while he steals from us.

In the same way, we can own our destiny by willingly surrendering to God (Revelations 3:20) or losing it to the devil. By not voluntarily submitting to God, we are automatically under the lordship of the devil, and he owns our destiny. Such is so because we exist in this world, which is governed by the god of this world, the devil (2 Corinthians 4:4). Unless we willfully put our destiny under God, we are under the god of this world for as long as we are in this world physically. Surrendering to God is the only thing that translates us out of this world while we live in this world. Thus, we are in the world but not of the world (John 17:16). This way, we are above the god of this world—the devil, thereby owning our destiny and attaining dominion. So, to own our destiny is to be translated above the world, rule over the god of this world, and attain dominion.

Lastly, the god of this world is a thief with a mission to steal, kill and destroy (John 10:10). As we all know, it is impossible to steal without distraction; therefore, distractions are a prolific weapon used by the devil. Whatever has nothing to do with our destiny does not deserve our focus and time—the goodness of it notwithstanding. The devil brings things to us that have nothing to do with our destiny but to get our attention away from something valuable; while distracted, he steals from us. We need to be aware of this and guard against every distraction. Before we engage in anything, seek God on it and locate the camouflage of the devil from far off.

In summary, one of the main reasons God made humans was so we can have dominion on earth (Genesis 1:26). When Adam messed up (Genesis 3), God sent Jesus to reset humanity back to the path of dominion (John 3:16). So, when dominion is not achieved, we have failed. Though there are over eight billion people on earth now, there is a place for each one of us to reign. In this book, we have shared many practical ways to attain dominion; however, to see results and to be on top as God has destined, we must *be doers of the word and not hearers only, deceiving ourselves* James 1:22.

Here are the crucial things that we must keep in mind as we walk through the path shown in this book:

1. We must locate our call. Life begins when we know the heart of the Father towards our creation. Until this is known, we are simply going through life on the devil's timetable as he steals, kills, and destroys us. There are many ways to do this, but the sure way is to consult our Maker.
2. Do only what God has called you to. As a creation of God, we are equipped for more. In Psalm 23:5, David described the blessings of God as overflowing. It means when God created us; He equipped us with overflowing grace. Then even as a believer, we have the Holy Spirit through Jesus Christ with whom we

can do all things (Philippians 4:13). However, not all things are beneficial to us (1 Corinthians 10:23). In other words, what we have not been sent to do will hurt what we have been sent to do; therefore, we must locate what is beneficial and drill down into it.
3. See every call as a mini destiny. Until we give account to God after life, we must see everything about life as temporary, see every call as an assignment with a time frame, and never get to the point of settlement. Such is because there is time for everything under heaven (Ecclesiastes 3:10), which includes our destinies.
4. Do not be ignorant of the vices of the devil (2 Corinthians 2:11). *Be sober, be vigilant; because your adversary, the devil, walks about like a roaring lion, seeking whom he may devour* (1 Peter 5:8). We must know what tactics the devil uses for us and our calling and also know our weaknesses and to seek help. What causes significant damage to you may not do the same for me. Samson's hair must not be cut off, but this was not the case for John the Baptist.
5. Rely on God. Since God created the heavens and the earth (Genesis 1:1), it is simply impossible to go through life and have overall success without Him (John 10:10). *Trust in the Lord with all your heart and lean not on your own understanding; In all your ways acknowledge Him, and He shall direct your paths.* Proverbs 3:5-6.

As you make up your mind to own your destiny by willingly surrendering it to God, I pray that God will empower you in Jesus' name. Amen.

New Believer's Prayer

Dear Heavenly Father,
I come to you a sinner in need of a savior. I believe that Jesus died for my sins, and You raised Him from the dead on the third day. Therefore, I confess Jesus as Lord and surrender to His Lordship. Fill me with your Holy Spirit and help me to obey You always. Thank you because now I know I am saved, and I ask that you help me to remain and grow in You all the days of my life in Jesus' name. Amen.

Contact the Author

I am sure this book has blessed you, and it will be my joy to hear from you. You can reach me at info@eagboola.com. For more information about me, please visit my website at www.eagboola.com.

Jesus Bless you.

About the Book

Destiny is God's vision for each individual to achieve here on earth. It is the reason for our creation. If you are alive today, then God envisioned a purpose for you to achieve. In this book, you will learn the different options available to all.

Contrary to common beliefs, destiny is not set in stone. Yes, God set a goal, purpose and plan for each creation. However, by creating humans in His image and giving us free will, God gave every individual the sovereignty to chart their course. Adam and Eve charted their course and suffered the consequences. So was Eli in 1 Samuel 2. However, we can only strive to achieve what we know. This book shows the practical steps to locate your purpose and work towards it.

Since destiny is the core of God's agenda for each person, getting a person out of God's ordination for their life is a significant aim of the devil. Therefore, the essence of this book becomes critical because sin, the only thing that separates humans from God, is simply going against God's ordination. You will learn the strategy used by the devil to achieve this in this book.

Finally, if God created us with a purpose, He expects us to fulfill that purpose. As such, He will hold us to that standard. On the last day, we will be evaluated on two fronts. First, are you of God? That is, born again? Such is what will determine where you end up—heaven or hell. You will learn the path to salvation in this book. Secondly, did you fulfill the destiny set before you by God? It will determine the treasures you will have in heaven. This book shows you how to ensure that you don't just make heaven but have great treasures in heaven.

If you are not saved, this book is for you. However, this book is also for you if you are saved and unsure what to pursue or how to pursue after God. There is a place carved out by God just for you. In this place, you can genuinely pursue God in an acceptable way. May you find that place as you read this book in Jesus' name. Amen.

Other Books By the Author

1. The Person You Should Know
2. The Most Important Act
3. The Most Important Person of Our Time
4. The Blueprint of Relationships
5. The Simplicity of Spirituality: An Introduction

Ebenezer Agboola is a teacher in the body of Christ by calling. The core of his call is to bring the light of understanding into the darkness of deception by teaching the word of God. He believes that ignorance is bondage and that understanding is freedom with its source from the Holy Spirit (2 Corinthians 3:17). Hence, his passion is seeing people seek understanding and apply it correctly (wisdom). The nature of his call makes him relevant not just to Christians but to everyone. He is a *Christian Apologist* whose passion is to bring the reality and practicality of God to reality.

He has authored books like The Person You Should Know, The Most Important Person of Our Time and various others to enhance growth in God. He is also the founding teaching minister of a teaching ministry called "The Ministry of Light international" (MOLI). The ministry organizes conferences and teaching events led by the Holy Spirit, where Ebenezer serves as the host minister.

He is happily married to Tumininu, and they are blessed with a lovely daughter Deborah.

www.ingramcontent.com/pod-product-compliance
Lightning Source LLC
Chambersburg PA
CBHW072054110526
44590CB00018B/3163